RED LETTER DAYS

A book of Holiday Customs

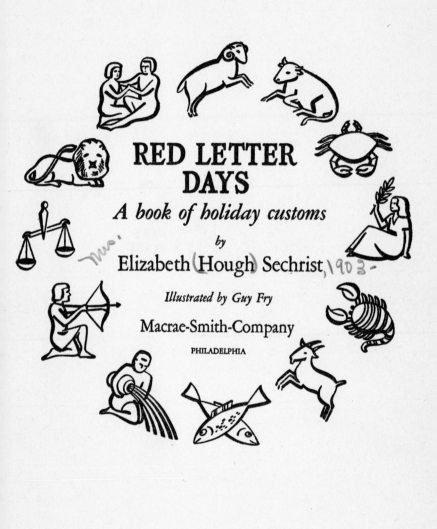

RED LETTER DAYS

A book of holiday customs

by

Elizabeth (Hough) Sechrist, 1903-

Illustrated by Guy Fry

Macrae-Smith-Company

PHILADELPHIA

Holidays

FIFTH PRINTING

405

Manufactured in the United States of America

TO MY SISTER

C. H. B.

" Of loyal nature and of noble mind "

65959

ACKNOWLEDGMENTS

THE *author wishes to thank the* ST. NICHOLAS MAGAZINE *for permission to use the material in the chapter on The Easter Season, based on her article published by them called "It's An Old Easter Custom"; Houghton, Mifflin Company for permission to quote from the poem "Decoration Day" by Henry Wadsworth Longfellow; the Curtis Publishing Company for permission to quote from "The Mother of Mother's Day" by Ann Hark published in the* COUNTRY GENTLEMAN; *and the U. S. Department of Agriculture for permission to use material from their publications: Arbor Day, and Famous Trees.*

For material on the Ukraine I am indebted to Mr. Vladimir Malevich of Pittsburgh and the UKRAINIAN WEEKLY *and its editor Mr. Stephen Shumeyko. I wish also to thank Miss Wava Clay for her invaluable assistance in my work at the Reference Department of the Carnegie Library of Pittsburgh. And to my authorities— eighty books and innumerable periodicals and pamphlets, I am greatly indebted.*

PREFACE

Holidays have been observed by all races and classes since ancient times. Indeed, it is not hard to imagine the cavemen of a prehistoric age celebrating some particularly successful hunting or fishing expedition by proclaiming a holiday! The impulse to make a momentous occasion of the anniversary of an important event seems almost instinctive to civilized man, and from historic records we know that anniversaries and red-letter days of all kinds have given us the holidays we celebrate today.

Many of our American holidays are comparatively young, but even a nation as new as our own is rich in tradition. Thanksgiving inherited from the Pilgrim Fathers, Independence Day commemorating the birth of our country, Columbus Day, Constitution Day, Flag Day,—all are identified with our early history. Armistice Day and Pan-American Day link us with other nations, while Christmas, Easter, and New Year's we share with mankind the world over. Days like St. Patrick's Day, St. Valentine's Day, May Day and Hallowe'en, though not legal holidays, have a definite place on our calendar because they have become so

[9]

enriched by centuries of custom that their observance has never ceased.

It is impossible to study the history of our holidays without being conscious of the history and growth of the peoples who observed them. Throughout the nations of the world certain days are observed which have a significance to that country alone, holidays that have developed with the nation. In this book it did not seem necessary to include any except those that were similar to or comparable with some holiday of our own. However, many of the holidays inherited from the Old World are colored with ancient customs reflecting the manners and customs of a world of the past,—the ancient Romans, the Celts of Britain, the Medieval English, and the peasants of Ireland, Scotland and Wales, as well as our own Colonial ancestors. When we observe these old holidays today we are keeping alive in the present the traditions of the past, for they have a foothold so firmly rooted that modern ways cannot push them completely from the calendar. Let us hope that it will be a long, long time before these colorful customs vanish. Long may they thrive!

ELIZABETH HOUGH SECHRIST.

York County, Pennsylvania
St. Valentine's Day, 1940.

CONTENTS

[11]

CONTENTS

RED LETTER DAYS

A book of Holiday Customs

STORY OF THE CALENDAR

For thousands of years, ever since the dawn of civilization, men have employed some method of measuring time.
Time has always been an important element in the lives
of men of all ages and races, and so, for convenience sake,
the calendar was invented. The word calendar comes from
the Roman *kalends* meaning the first of the month, but calendars were in use for many centuries before the Roman
Empire. In the time of the Ancient Egyptians a solar year
was worked out by the shadows cast by those ageless won-
ders, the pyramids. And even before the beginning of actual
recorded history we know there must have been various ways
of counting the succession of days and months and years,
this "Chequerboard of Nights and Days," as Omar

Khayyám so appropriately expressed it nearly a thousand years ago.

Counting nights instead of days was a custom of the Ancient Germans. From them has come the term fortnight, fourteen nights. Their calendar included no months and only three seasons, for autumn was omitted entirely in their division of the year. Instead of days they used tides as a measure, sixty tides to a month. About one hundred years before the time of Christ, the Teutonic races accepted the Roman or pre-Julian calendar.

The first Roman calendar that we know anything about, supposed to have been created by Numa Pompilius in the seventh century B. C., usually contained about 304 days. In order to bring their time up to the correct solar year, an extra month was added every now and then by the priests to the tenth month, for ten months with weeks consisting of eight days each comprised this old calendar. About three hundred years before the time of the Cæsars, this calendar was amended by Cnæus Flavius. However, in Cicero's time the calendar was inaccurate by six weeks, and in Julius Cæsar's time by two months! No wonder, then, that Cæsar found it to be unsatisfactory. It was he who set about making real reforms, giving us the basis of the calendar we use today.

By Cæsar's reckoning there were 365¼ days in the solar year, so he arranged to have an extra day every four years to take care of this odd six hours a year. The extra day was added by observing February the 24th *twice* in Leap Year. But in order to bring the calendar up to date with the sun he added two months to the year we now refer to as 46 B. C., inserting them between the months of November and December. The year of the new calendar's adoption therefore was the longest year on record; it contained 445 days! However, from the time the new Julian Calendar really went into effect until the year 1582, no changes were made and it worked remarkably well considering the inefficiency of previous calendars!

At the time Julius Cæsar began his calendar reforms there were only 355 days in the year. To these he added ten more in this wise: two at the end of January, August, and December; one at the end of April, June, July and September. Have you ever wondered why there are thirty-one days in both July and August, the only two long months that come together, and why February is so short? The answer is that a day was taken from February and added to August, to make it contain as many days as July, so that the month named for Augustus Cæsar should not seem inferior to the month named for Julius.

With the irregularity of the length of our months, it is fortunate that someone made up a verse as a reminder of the number of days contained in each.

Thirty days hath September,
April, June and November,
All the rest have thirty-one,
Except February alone
Which has twenty-eight and one more
Added every year in four.

With the exception of changing the month of *Quinctilus*
to July and the month *Sextilis* to August, the names of the
months remained as they had been, as follows:

March —named for Mars, Roman god of war.
April —from the Latin " aperio "—to open.
May —uncertainty as to whether from the little-known
goddess Maia, or the word " maior "—increas-
ing.
June —probably from Juno, though historians differ
on this.
July —for Julius Cæsar.
August —for Augustus Cæsar.
September —7th month (in the Roman calendar).
October —8th month.
November —9th month.
December —10th month.
January —from the ancient Roman god of beginnings.
February —from Latin word " februum "—an instrument
of purification. According to authorities the
god Februus superseded the naming of the
month.

Each month in the Roman Calendar had three important days—the Kalends or first of the month, the Nones or fifth, and the Ides or thirteenth. But to these there were exceptions as the verse explains.

March, July, October, May
Make Nones the seventh, Ides the fifteenth day.

Because of the fact that Julius Cæsar was slain on the Ides of March which came on the fifteenth day, and probably also because of the familiar quotation from Shakespeare's *Julius Caesar,* " Beware of the Ides of March," we are apt to think of the Ides as having been the fifteenth in every Roman month, instead of the exception.

The Roman week contained eight days, with seven working days ending in a big market day called the *nundina.* Originally Jewish, the seven-day week was not adopted in Rome until after the introduction of Christianity. Even then, after a time, the people went back again to the eight-day week. It was not until Christianity had a strong foothold throughout the civilized world that the seven-day week came to stay.

In studying the names of the days of the week we can see that several languages and peoples influenced their naming, though the origin of their names is distinctly pagan.

Because of their pagan origin, the days of the week and the months are numbered instead of named by the Society of Friends.

Sunday comes from *sunnan daeg,* Anglo-Saxon for sun day. Likewise Monday is derived from moon day, *mona daeg.* Tuesday is for Tyr, Norse god of war, or, in the Anglo-Saxon, *Tiwes daeg.* Wednesday is *Wodin's daeg* for the Norse god of storms, Odin, and Thursday for the Norse god of thunder, Thor. Friday was named for Thor's wife, Freya. Saturday gets its name from the Roman god of the harvest, Saturn, which in Anglo-Saxon is *Saeterdaeg.*

The custom of dating the years of the Christian era from the year of Christ's birth as A. D.—*Anno Domini* (in the year of our Lord) and the time before Christ, B. C.—was conceived by a churchman of the sixth century, Abbott Dionysius Exigus, by name. But somewhere, somehow, an error was made in the reckoning, and historians believe that Christ was really born some time between the years 9 and 7 B. C. The exact date will never be known. Likewise the day and month are not known exactly. For many years at the beginning of the Christian era, both November 17th and March 28th were sought to be placed as the time of His birth, unsuccessfully. In the year 354 A. D. the Roman Bishop Liberius began to celebrate Christ's birthday on December 25th and that date has been kept ever since.

Although the calendar as Julius Cæsar had made it was very nearly accurate, and is used to this day with some few exceptions, that slight inaccuracy threw it off, after several hundred years. When the year 1582 rolled around, the calendar was ten days behind the sun and Pope Gregory

decided to do something about it. So he dropped the ten days! Julius Cæsar had reckoned 365¼ days to a year, but the year actually contains something less than he had figured; to be exact, the earth goes round the sun in 365 days, 5 hours, 48 minutes and 46 seconds! With the passing of centuries this inaccuracy had amounted to a difference more serious than the Roman emperor could have foreseen.

After some calculations, Pope Gregory decided that a Leap Year dropped every now and then from the calendar would correct the difficulty. His figuring resulted in this conclusion: that every year divisible by 4 should be a leap year *except* when it was divisible by 100. But he made an exception to that rule, too, deciding that those years that are divisible by 400 should *be* a Leap Year, whether or no! In other words, the year 1600 was a leap year, the years 1700, 1800, 1900 were not. But the year 2000 will be a leap year because it is divisible by 400. In this way, and still observing the rule of "every year in four" the Gregorian Calendar has been called correct except for an additional 26 seconds every year! But since these additional seconds cannot total a full day until 3323 years have passed, there is little to worry about in the Gregorian Calendar as far as inaccuracies are concerned.

Although Pope Gregory's new calendar was accepted by Rome and made lawful in an act dated March 1, 1582, it was not until 1752 that Great Britain finally adopted it, at which time eleven days had to be dropped. In that year the dates in England went like this—September 1, 2, 14, 15, etc. Anyone whose birthday fell on a date between the 2d and 14th of September had to wait until the following year to celebrate it! But with the adoption of the Gregorian Calendar, the calendars of Great Britain were in line with most of the European countries that had been using the Gregorian for years. Scotland, for instance, had adopted it in 1600. Today the Gregorian is the national calendar of most countries of the civilized world. However, many people still use the Julian in reckoning their holidays. And for their church festivals various ancient calendars are still adhered to.

Probably the oldest calendar still in use is the Hindu, in existence at least five centuries before the birth of Christ, and still used in many parts of India today.

It is interesting to know that there is still in common use a calendar that has been the same for nearly six thousand years. The ancient Hebrew Calendar of Biblical times is the same one that is used by Orthodox Jews today. Based on a lunar year, there is a difference of more than eleven days between it and the solar year. In order to " catch up " with the sun's year the Hebrew Calendar adds a month, Adar Sheni, seven times in every nineteen years. The inaccuracy lies in the fact that twelve moons (a lunar year) do not quite make a solar year. The flexibility of the Hebrew Calendar makes the feasts and holidays come at different times every year on the modern calendar. New Year's, *Rosh Hashana,* in 1939 came on September 14–15; in 1940 on October 3–4. Likewise *Yom Kippur,* the Day of Atonement, was September 23 in 1939, and on October 12 in 1940.

The Jewish festivals are the oldest on record. Many of them are symbolic of the pastoral life led by the Hebrews in ancient times. To study their holidays and their origin is to recognize the historic tradition of their race. Most important of all these is *Yom Kippur.* The ten days between *Rosh Hashana* and *Yom Kippur* are known as the Days of Penitence. Other important festivals are the *Pesach* or Passover, coming about the time of our Easter and commemorating the exodus of the Children of Israel from the land of Egypt; also *Shabouth* the Feast of Weeks, and *Succoth* the Feast of Tabernacles.

The Mohammedan Calendar begins its year in December. Adopted in the year 622 A. D., it was put into effect by the great prophet Mohammed, founder of the Islam religion. Although used today by the people of that faith, most of the Mohammedans use the Gregorian Calendar in their secular life.

For a short time in France a different calendar was tried out but found unsatisfactory. Adopted October 5, 1793, after the French Revolution, it was abolished on December 31, 1805, when the Gregorian Calendar was once more established. Known as the Republican and also the Revolutionary Calendar, it had twelve months of thirty days each, with five or six days added at the end of the year to make it agree with the solar year; not a very convenient arrangement.

Since 1923 there have been serious movements toward
instituting a new calendar, one that could be used by all
countries of the world. A Calendar Council of the League
of Nations worked for years on calendar reforms, and it is
said that nearly two hundred proposals were made. To date
none has been accepted. However, there are two worth
mentioning here because both were considered; the last, a
World Calendar, having been approved by a Council of
fourteen nations. The first was a thirteen month calendar of
28 days each, each month to contain exactly four weeks.
As this would total only 364 days, an extra day would come
at the end of the year to be known as "year day"; likewise
every four years a "leap day" would be observed between
June and Sol. Sol, being the name of the extra, or thirteenth
month, would come between June and July.

The other proposed calendar, and the one most favored,
has less drastic changes from the present one. Miss Elisabeth
Achelis, founder and president of the World Calendar
Association, is its foremost advocate. This World Calendar
would contain twelve months divided into equal quarters
of three months each, the first month of each quarter would
contain thirty-one days, the other two, thirty days each. This
calendar, too, it is proposed, should have a day at the end
of the year, the 365th, known as Year End Day, and a Leap
Day between June and July every fourth year. The first day

of the quarter would always be Sunday. With this arrangement, Christmas and New Year's would always come on a week-end, a great advantage to all working people. Another immense advantage, especially to bookkeepers and payroll clerks, is the fact that all months would contain twenty-six working days. Since each quarter would have exactly the same length, comparisons could be made in business statistics that have been tremendously difficult with the present calendar.

Whether or not a World Calendar is adopted depends upon a great many factors. There are unquestionably many advantages from the standpoint of efficiency, convenience and international unity. On the other hand, our present method of reckoning time, with only slight changes, is about two thousand years old, and custom dies hard. Involved in so drastic a change are tradition, custom, and even superstition. But the people of Cæsar's time got used to a new calendar, and the British finally surrendered their Julian Calendar, in spite of much bitter opposition, in favor of the Gregorian. If a new calendar is adopted within our time we will, undoubtedly, do as well as they in adjusting ourselves to the change.

January 1

NEW YEAR'S DAY

*" This is the year that for you waits
Beyond tomorrow's mystic gates."*
—Horatio Nelson Powers.

Time, moving along unceasingly, waits for no man, linking the years together in an endless chain. When New Year's Eve comes and the clock strikes the last hour of the last day of the old year, we feel ourselves being carried along on the tide of time, looking ahead hopefully to the new year that lies before us. Another January First, another beginning!

The new year has not always begun on January first. In Ancient Egypt thousands of years ago, the year began at the time of the overflowing of the River Nile which occurred about the middle of June. The early Romans began their year in March just as the Ancient Babylonians had done long before them, but it was a famous Roman who changed the date of New Year's to January first. The Julian Calendar, Julius Cæsar's new method of reckoning time, was a forerunner of our own. In Anglo-Saxon England the 21st of December was New Year's Day until William the Conqueror changed it to January first. England was to know other New Year's Days, however, for later March 25th was observed, along with other nations of the world; then in 1752 England adopted the Gregorian Calendar and January first again, this time permanently, as New Year's.

The Romans have been given credit for the origin of giving gifts at New Year's, a custom practiced in some countries today. It is said that Augustus Cæsar claimed to have had a vision in which he saw himself receiving gifts from the Senate and the people on the Kalends of January. In England at the time of Queen Elizabeth there was a special ceremony at Court for exchanging presents. Historians claim that practically all of Queen Elizabeth's wardrobe and jewelry came to her as New Year's gifts. It was about this time that the term " pin-money " originated. After the invention of this useful article, when money was given to the ladies at New Year's it was called pin-money because they were so intrigued with pins that this would, in all probability, be the object of their spending!

An important feature of New Year's Day in early England was the Wassail Bowl. A drink called *lamb's wool* was carefully blended in the large Wassail Bowl then handed around to every member of the family, each person wishing the other " Wass hael! "—" To your health! " Also made especially for New Year's consumption were the popular god-cakes, cut into triangles of all sizes and filled with wholesome mince-meat filling.

In the olden days New Year's was considered a good time to foretell the future, to look ahead into the year just beginning. One custom was known as " dipping." The family Bible was read by the master of the house. He opened the book with eyes closed and the passage found by his finger indicated the fortune of his house for the ensuing year. The text was read solemnly and interpreted by the family as a prognostication of the luck, good or ill, that would befall.

Probably the most wide-spread of all New Year's superstitions and one that was taken most seriously was that concerning the " first-footer! " The type of person who first set foot in the house on the first day of the year was considered extremely important. For instance, it was very bad

luck for a woman to enter one's house first on New Year'
Day, and unlucky for the first-footer to be a light-haired
man. Among others considered unlucky were grave-diggers
persons who walked with their toes turned in, those whose
eyebrows met, and men with red or blond hair! In many
villages, in order to avoid any catastrophe such an occur-
rence might bring upon an innocent household, a dark
haired man was chosen as a first-footer and his job was to
go from house to house where he would be first to enter
preserving the good fortune of the house. If everybody who
entered on the first day of the year carried food into the
house, that was considered good luck. Among the peasants
there was such a fear of starvation that a peculiar ceremony
was practiced in many homes to ward off this stark enemy
" Breaking the cake " it was called. A special New Year's
cake was dashed with much force against the door, then
everybody rushed to pick up a piece and eat it, praying
meanwhile that neither hunger nor want should enter that
house. It was considered very bad luck to throw anything
out on this day, even if it were ashes or a bit of rubbish!
Superstitious people were filled with untold dread if, by
accident or forgetfulness, someone carried from the house
a light or a candle, for this, they believed, meant death to a
member of that household before the year was past.

" Burning out the old year " by building huge bonfires

o which everybody added fuel, is still observed on New
Year's Eve in many parts of England and Scotland. In Sussex
here is an old custom of throwing apples, oranges and nuts
out the window to be scrambled for by the fishermen of
he town. A quaint custom said to have persisted from the
ime of the Druids is practiced in Northumberland; twenty-
four men dressed in old-time costumes march around the
own from eleven-thirty until midnight with pans of blazing
ar on their heads. The children of Northumberland beg
or gifts of coins on New Year's Day, saying, "Old Year
out, New Year in, please give us a New Year's gift."

In Scotland where New Year's Day is often known as
Hogmanay, the children go in a procession from house to
house on Hogmanay Eve asking for oat bread and cheese.

> *"Get up, good wife, and shake your feathers,*
> *And dinna think that we are beggars;*
> *For we are bairns come out to play,*
> *Get up and gie's our Hogmanay."*

The Monday after New Year's, known as Handsel Monday,
is a big day in the life of the boys and girls in Scotland, for
it is the day when they receive their gifts. Besides, it is the
day of a feast, and on every table there is sure to be found
plenty of the special cakes that are made by the good house-

wives of Scotland,—oaten cakes and wheat cakes, all dec orated, many of them bearing the greetings: " A merri auld Yule! "

In France, as in Scotland, New Year's is the importar holiday of the year when gifts are exchanged. All day th doorbells ring, for besides those who leave packages ther are the tradesmen who come to the door and wish the peopl of the house " *Bonne anée!* " and receive, in turn, gifts o money. There is a most joyous atmosphere among the peopl of this happy nation at the holiday season, an abundanc of goodwill with feasting, drinking each other's health an much gayety. New Year's gifts are proudly displayed for th many callers who come and go throughout the day. And ye the *Jour de l'an* has its serious side, too. New Year's Ev is also the Vigil of St. Sylvester, and the churches are gen erally crowded, while in some of the remote country place there is a quaint custom, on this Eve of Sylvester, of drivin, the cattle to the door of the church where the priest say Mass for their protection for the year to follow. Anothe custom in France is the visiting of graves by the familie of the departed ones, since this day is thought to be a goo time to remember the dead as well as the living.

New Year's Eve in Switzerland is also celebrated a Sylvester Day. On that day the children call the lazy one o the family, or the one who is last out of bed, a " Sylvester! "

The Armenians' New Year is much like our Christmas. There it is customary for friends of the family to lower a basket of gifts down the chimney!

St. Basil's Day is celebrated in Greece on January first in honor of St. Basil who was Bishop of Cæsarea in the fourth century. On that day the carollers go about singing songs and carrying a miniature "St. Basil's ship" to represent the boat on which the Saint sailed from Cæsarea. The Greeks also have Basil-cakes which everyone eats on New Year's,— round, flat savory morsels. The baking of these cakes is a traditional ceremony, even the wealthiest of the Greek women performing this task with their own hands, and donning their very best clothes and jewelry for the occasion. The master of the house makes the sign of the cross as he cuts the cake. Happy is that member of the family who finds the small silver coin that has been placed therein, for great good luck is believed in store for the one whose cake contains it!

Roumania is another country that combines the St. Basil celebration with the New Year's. On New Year's Eve young people go about from house to house, ringing bells, cracking whips, and singing songs of New Year's greetings. On the next day these greetings are continued and the people throw corn at each other for good luck.

To the people of the Far East the first day of the New

Year is very important indeed. Japanese bells ring out 108 times, as a reminder of the 108 commandments of Buddha, at midnight in the Buddhist temples, ushering in the New Year. The holiday was formerly celebrated for two weeks, but now that the Gregorian Calendar has been adopted by the Japanese nation, the longer celebration is not so universally observed. However, many of the ancient customs still prevail. One of these is the practice of scattering parched beans to the four corners of the house so that the devils will be driven from the place and good luck will enter. Then a straw rope is tied across the door to keep out all evil! The housewives will have been very busy getting ready for the holiday. The house is cleaned from top to bottom and the broom tied up so that no sweeping can be done on New Year's Day, for this might frighten away the good spirits! Another task of the Japanese housewife is to secure sacred coals from the temple with which to start her fire to cook the New Year's dinner. Certain symbolic dishes are served on specific days of the New Year festival. For instance, on the third day, small hard rice cakes—*mochi*—are eaten with a special good-luck tea and preserved plums. The plum denotes old age, the significance being that those who eat the plum will be blessed with long life. On the seventh day all partake of the "gruel of the seven herbs" to rid the mind and body of evil during the year to come.

After having used the lunar calendar for more than 4000 years, the Chinese as well as the Japanese have begun to observe January first as New Year's, showing the Occidental influence in the East. New Year's in China is distinctly a time of friendship and goodwill. Celebrations are in the home where the family sit at a round table so that the family circle will be, and remain, unbroken. Many of the old Chinese customs are still observed by some, though many of the modern Chinese have dropped the significant and meaningful customs of their forefathers. Making calls on New Year's Day is thought to have originated with the Chinese, a custom that is now observed in many lands by millions of people. The people of China and Japan can call on their friends with a clear conscience, for in those countries they start the new year with a clean slate. It is an integral part of their religion to pay *all* debts before the stroke of midnight on the last day of the year!

Another custom common to China and Japan is that of adding a year to one's age on New Year's Day! Besides being the birthday of the year, it is the birthday of every person,—man, woman, or child, in the land!

Eating seven dinners on the last day of the year is a ritual with the Mongols, and an enjoyable one for these hardy people who ordinarily eat once a day. In Mongolia New Year's Day is called " The First of the White Month."

It depends upon your religion, as to when you observe the year's birthday in India, though many Hindus do observe it January first. A unique custom there is that of handing your friends a lime or lemon on New Year's Day. Consequently, the fruit markets do an immense business the week preceding the holiday. Many people keep a basket beside their door which piles high with the fruit before the day is over. Natives of the same caste present each other with flowers and wreaths to be worn around the neck.

March twenty-first is New Year's Day for the Persians; they celebrate it for two full weeks. It is deemed most important for the homes to be spic-and-span and for everybody to have new clothes to wear on the holiday. To insure happiness for all the family, seven foods beginning with the letter " s " are included in the New Year's dinner. The Persians present each other with eggs, the symbol of the beginning of life.

To the Jewish people the New Year is known as the Head of the Year, the day as *Rosh Hashana*. On that day every Jew is called to account for all his deeds throughout the year; those who deserve it, to have their names written in the Book of Life; those who are entirely discreditable, to be eternally condemned; but those who are not entirely on the wrong path may have nine days of grace in which to perform good deeds. This period of time is up at Yom

Kippur, the Day of Atonement. A twenty-four hour fast precedes Yom Kippur ending at sunset when a trumpet sounds, signifying the closing of the Book of Life. Candles are burned during this time of fast in the homes of every Orthodox Jew, while many spend the hours at prayer in the synagogue.

When compared with customs of other countries throughout the world, our New Year's Day here in America seems to be one of events rather than of tradition. A huge parade, a nationally-heralded football game, a rose festival, these and many other events are fast becoming customs in this country. One of these is the historic President's Reception at the White House, an annual event that started the first year America had a president. New Year's calls were almost unheard of in colonial times anywhere except New York City, and when George Washington went to New York as President of the new republic, he was pleasantly surprised at the custom. On that first New Year's Day the President and Mrs. Washington started the custom that has been kept up ever since.

It used to be the practice in New York City, around the time of the " Gay Nineties " when much entertaining was done, for the newspapers to publish a list of the people in the city who would receive callers on New Year's Day. The names filled several columns. Making calls on the first day of the new year even in New York is not nearly so popular as it used to be, but the custom dies hard and many people still " go the rounds."

Carnivals are very popular in the South where the weather is warm and the people are carnival-minded. But the southerners are not the only ones who have New Year's carnivals and parades. One of the most famous parades in the country is that held by the " Mummers " in Philadelphia. The origin of this parade goes back to colonial times when Swedish settlers used to observe New Year's by masquerading and going about town, gay and hilarious, to celebrate the New Year in what they considered an appropriate manner. These bands of mummers were finally organized in 1876, and in 1901 they were given their first permits to parade. The members of the organization, consisting of many different clubs throughout the city, compete for prizes. The most spectacular costumes in the parade are worn by the presidents of the clubs,—costumes that are almost grotesque in their gorgeousness and immensity. Some of them weigh so much that it is a problem for the wearer to walk the long miles of city streets, lined with hundreds of thousands of spectators.

The parade of the Mummers in Philadelphia is usually made through icy streets on a typical Eastern seaboard winter day, while on the same day in Pasadena, California, another parade is in progress featuring sunshine and roses! This is the Tournament of Roses, a magnificent display of roses of all colors and kinds, in all shapes and figures. Floats are covered with them in the form of boats and ships and airplanes and furniture and houses and gardens, attended by men, women, boys and girls, covered with fragrant blossoms. Since 1866 the Pasadena Tournament of Roses has been an Association that produces, year after year, one of the most amazing processions in the United States. The Rose Bowl in Pasadena is the center of interest on New Year's for all sport fans, for it is the scene each year of an important football game between the leading team of the Pacific Coast, and one representing another section of the country.

The warm sunny climate of Mexico makes this a country of fairs, carnivals and festivals. The Mexicans love music, dancing, and the sunny outdoors, and all these can be had in plenty at a carnival. New Year's Day finds the people of Mexico enjoying fairs all over the land, with rodeos, bullfights and cockfights, plays and outdoor pageants, parades and races. It is a holiday to be enjoyed.

" This is the year that for you waits," the poet says. And, conversely, we wait for the new year! People all over the world are waiting for that last long minute of the old year to tick out, for the last grain of sand in the hour-glass to fall, for the last dying breath of the year that is done. Then at last that very second has arrived,—it is twelve o'clock and the New Year stands on the threshold, peering in at us. Clocks in village, town and city are striking the hour while church bells are pealing, whistles in the cities and on the ships in the harbor are blowing, and everywhere at every corner and in every place where there are people, horns are tooted and tin pans beat merrily. Somewhere off in the distance a cannon booms. The New Year has been shot in, and men, women and children from every walk of life shout gladly to each other, "Happy New Year!"

February 12
LINCOLN'S BIRTHDAY

Every school child knows the life of Abraham Lincoln, from the house of his birth built crudely of logs, down to the White House in Washington where he spent his last years; of his career as storekeeper to lawyer, lawyer to Congressman, Congressman to President; and of his tragic death at the close of the war. There is so much in the life of Lincoln to kindle inspiration in the hearts of young Americans that none can afford to miss reading his entire story. Of all the great Americans, his life is probably the most popular with young and old alike.

Emancipator of a race, martyr to a great cause, believer in the right, today his memory is cherished by every true 'American. There are many portraits and statues of Lincoln so that his likeness is familiar to all. Abraham Lincoln described his appearance in a short biography of himself with these words: " If any personal description of me is thought desirable, it may be said I am in height six feet four inches, nearly; lean in flesh, weighing, on an average, one hundred and eighty pounds; dark complexion, with coarse black hair and gray eyes—no other marks or brands recollected." Lincoln was by nature a retiring man, modest and humble. His shy manner was sometimes mistaken for rudeness while he lived, but all who really knew the man knew his great, kind heart, incapable of rudeness. Lincoln was never known to give deliberate offense to anyone.

As is so often the case with great personages, Lincoln's true worth, his extreme brilliance and clearsightedness as a statesman, were not truly appreciated until after his death. Since then many biographies have been written about him, and Lincoln's own writings have become world-famous. Abe the boy, Lincoln the man, Lincoln, statesman and president, have come alive in the words and by the pen of those who knew him or have made exhaustive studies of his life.

Everything of interest because of its connection with Abraham Lincoln has become touched with tradition and monetary value. One of the most outstanding collections of Lincolniana was the Osborn H. Oldroyd Collection. Mr. Oldroyd through his entire lifetime collected objects which had to do with the life of Lincoln. The collection was housed in a red brick building, an old boarding-house, across the street from the Ford Theatre where Lincoln was fatally shot. In 1926 when Mr. Oldroyd was an old man, he presented his precious collection to the Federal Government. Each piece of the many hundreds of objects in the collection was endeared to this old collector's heart because of its association with his hero.

Another notable contribution to Lincolniana is that given to the Library of Congress in Washington by his son, Robert Todd Lincoln. A large collection of letters, manuscripts, and papers, it was given with the provision that it should not be opened for inspection until twenty-one years after his death. Lincoln's son's gift will be available to the world in July, 1947. Mr. Lincoln began depositing his father's papers in the Library of Congress in 1919. When in 1922 he completed the collection, he presented it to the Library of Congress with a deed which provided that " all of said letters, manuscripts, documents and other papers shall be placed in a sealed vault or compartment and carefully preserved from official or public inspection or private view until the expiration of twenty-one years from the date of my death." The collection fills twenty-six filing cases and is thought to contain mostly letters *to* Lincoln. Letters from Lincoln have been used in great number by two of his greatest biographers, John G. Nicolay, private Secretary to President Lincoln, and his Secretary of State John Hay.

Aside from books that have told Lincoln's story, and many portraits of the tall, strong, homely character, there are shrines to Lincoln throughout the nation that are further proof of his endearment to the hearts of his countrymen. Probably the most beautiful of all these is the Lincoln Memorial erected in the nation's capital. Dedicated in 1922, it was built at a cost of three million dollars. The remarkably fine statue of Lincoln seated in a chair, done by the sculptor Daniel Chester French, is the center of the memorial.

Because of their importance as noted objects of sculpture in America, and because they contribute much to the memory of Lincoln, some of his shrines are listed below:

Lincoln's Tomb at Springfield, Illinois.
Memorial near his birthplace at Hodgenville, Kentucky.
St. Gaudens' Seated Lincoln at Grant Park, Chicago, Illinois.
St. Gaudens' Lincoln Standing, Westminster, London.
George Gray Bernard statue, original in Cincinnati, Ohio,
    with copies in Manchester, England and Louisville, Ky.
Gutzon Borglum's amazing figure of Lincoln at Newark,
    N. J., seated on a bench, his hat beside him, so life-
    like that children often believe it is real.

The small village in Illinois where Lincoln served as storekeeper and courted Ann Rutledge was recreated by

William Randolph Hearst in 1918 at the New Salem State Park and presented to the State of Illinois. In 1931 Nancy Hanks' cabin was dedicated at Harrodsburg, Kentucky, in memory of the time 125 years before when Nancy Hanks and Thomas Lincoln were married and made the little log cabin their home in the first white settlement west of the Allegheny Mountains.

Probably the first institution to be named for Abraham Lincoln was the Lincoln Memorial University at Harrodgate, Tennessee. It was founded in 1863 at the instigation of Lincoln. Another college taking his name was Lincoln Institute in Missouri for the training of negroes. It was started in 1866 with a fund of five thousand dollars raised by the Sixty-Second Colored Infantry!

Probably the most traveled highway in the world is the Lincoln Highway. Stretching across the United States from the Atlantic to the Pacific, from New York to San Francisco, it is 3,384 miles long.

The newest memorial to Lincoln is that tremendous piece of sculpture at Mt. Rushmore in South Dakota being executed by the famous sculptor, Gutzon Borglum. When completed the figure of Lincoln, far to the right, will stand with George Washington, Thomas Jefferson and Theodore Roosevelt. The head of the Lincoln figure was completed in 1937 and unveiled on September 17th of that year. The idea for this stupendous sculpturing feat was conceived by Doane Robinson in 1924. Said to be the greatest piece of work of its kind since the era of the ancient Egyptians, the four figures of Washington, Jefferson, Lincoln and Roosevelt standing at the gigantic proportions of 465 feet tall, are intended " to perpetuate the founding, the expansion, the preservation and the unification of the United States."

Lincoln's Birthday was first observed ten months after his death in 1866 in Washington, D. C., at which time a memorial address was made at a combined meeting of the House and Senate in formal commemoration of his tragic death. It was not until 1891 that the suggestion was made that Lincoln's Birthday should be made a national holiday. The following year the State of Illinois made February twelfth a legal holiday; several other states followed suit, and then year after year other states were added to those which observed Lincoln's Birthday. In 1940 it was legal in twenty-eight states and proclaimed a holiday in Massachusetts by the Governor. On the one hundredth anniversary of his birth—1909—there were celebrations all over America in honor of Abraham Lincoln, for by that time the bitterness of the South had melted into respect for a truly great man. That year, another famous American made the principal address at a Lincoln celebration in New York City. He was Booker T. Washington, a negro who had been given freedom and the right to live because of Abraham Lincoln and the Emancipation Proclamation.

The one hundred and thirtieth anniversary of Lincoln's birth was observed in 1939 by the dedication of a new memorial at Mt. Pulaski, Illinois, where the young lawyer had often " argued law " as a circuit rider.

Annually in the tiny town of Hingham, near Norwich, England, a service is held to honor Abraham Lincoln on his birthday. Hingham is justly proud of the bust of Lincoln which was given by Americans to the little Hingham Church. Its inscription reads: *" In this parish for many generations lived the Lincolns, ancestors of the American ABRAHAM LINCOLN. To Him, greatest of that lineage."* Lincoln's ancestry has been traced back to one Robert Lincoln who died in Hingham in 1543. It was this man's great-grandson Samuel who emigrated to the American Colonies in 1637 and became a weaver at Hingham, Massachusetts, and it was Samuel's grandson, John, who was killed by Indians leaving a five-year-old son, Thomas. Thomas Lincoln was Abraham's father.

Although it was his fate to be at the helm when this nation was launched upon the most tragic era of its career, Abraham Lincoln was far from being a warrior. He was a peace-loving man in every sense of the word, but his belief in peace was founded on his faith in the right. He believed slavery was not right. " As I would not be a slave, so I would not be a master," he said. He believed that the Union could be saved only by settling the question of slavery. No one dreaded more than he the issue toward which the slave problem was drawing the nation. But Lincoln knew, with his keen sense of foresight, that the Union would be dissolved if its differences were not settled once and for all. It was truly a question of " United we stand, divided we fall! " Even as it had been in the War of Independence! In an address at Cleveland, Ohio, in 1861 Lincoln made this clear when he said: " If we do not make common cause to save the good old ship of the Union on this voyage, nobody will have a chance to pilot her on another voyage."

The Civil War was unquestionably Lincoln's great tragedy. His heart ached for every man on the battlefields, whether he was fighting for the North or the South. Every casualty was, to him, another drop of blood spilled to blot the history of a valiant new country. Lincoln's speech at Gettysburg testified what he hoped for in the ultimate outcome of the struggle. Those words with which he ended his speech, immortalized by their greatness, signify his faith in what that outcome was to be: " That this nation, under God, shall have a new birth of freedom, and that government of the people, by the people, for the people, shall not perish from the earth."

Lincoln did at least live to see the end of the War and to see his faith in freedom rewarded. But his joy was short-lived. On April 15, 1865, after having been shot at Ford's Theatre by John Wilkes Booth, he died in his fifty-seventh year.

But the memory of Abraham Lincoln did not die. It has lived on in the hearts of the people of his country and of all the world; his ideals as well as his accomplishments, the things he said as well as what he did. Lincoln was wrong about one statement he made. In his address at Gettysburg he told his listeners: "The world will little note, nor long remember, what we say here." This speech of Lincoln's is far more likely to be remembered hundreds of years from now than any Battle of the Civil War. It, like Lincoln, had the substance of true immortality.

IMPORTANT DATES IN THE LIFE OF LINCOLN

1809—Born February 12th in State of Kentucky.

1816—Was moved to Indiana where he helped build log cabin.

1830—Moved to Illinois. Started law career there. Became Postmaster.

1842—Married Mary Todd of Lexington, Ky.

1847—Elected to Illinois State Congress.

1857—Famous debate with Douglas wherein he brought the slavery question to the fore.

1860—Nominated in Chicago for President by the Republican Party and elected that November.

1863—Gettysburg Speech, November 19th.

1864—Abolishment of slavery.

1865—On April 14th in Ford's Theatre shot by John Wilkes Booth. April 15th he died.

February 14

ST. VALENTINE'S DAY

Roses are red, violets are blue,
Sugar is sweet, and so are you!

That is a very, very old Valentine rhyme which, as children, we printed dozens of times. On the day before the 14th of February we made valentines galore for Valentine's Day. We achieved surprising results with old wallpaper, a paste-pot, and pictures cut from magazines and post-cards. Some-where on the valentine we always printed a verse, and on the back, ungrammatically, the words: *From guess who.* A big cardboard box with a huge slit in the top held these numerous, gay missives until St. Valentine's Day when, at the dinner table, the box was opened and the valentines distributed. Added to these were real "store valentines" from older members of the family, decorated with red hearts, paper-lace, cupids and loving verses suitable to the day.

Valentine boxes are still popular with American children, for valentines come cheap at a penny and boys and girls buy them by the dozens. Children in the grade schools have their valentine boxes, from which the valentines are distributed at the close of school, while they send others by mail. Among the grown-ups, boxes of candy decorated with big red hearts are more popular, and parties and dances are the custom on St. Valentine's Day, but for the most part February 14th has lost much of the romantic character it had in the olden days.

In times gone by, valentines sometimes cost as much as ten dollars apiece, and gorgeously extravagant creations they were, to be sure! One of these is described in a London magazine, "in which a white-enameled Cupid appeared with wings picked out in silver amid a network of balusters, tassels, escallop-shells, seaweed, and monster tulips"! About the time of the Civil War in America the valentine was at the height of its popularity, with young and old alike. A Boston periodical of 1863 says: "Indeed, with the excep-

tion of Christmas there is no festival throughout the year
which is invested with half the interest belonging to this
cherished anniversary."

Who started all this valentine-sending which has been
going on through hundreds of years, and who was St.
Valentine, anyway?

Many hundreds of years ago in the days of the Roman
festivals to pagan gods, there was a feast called the Luper-

calia, celebrated in honor of the gods Juno and Pan. It was
the custom at this feast for the young Romans to put into
a box the names of young maidens and then draw the names
out by chance. The girl whose name was chosen became the

young man's partner for the Lupercalia Festival. With the introduction of Christianity, all these pagan rites, because they were done in honor of heathen gods, were eradicated in every way possible. But the people had become so accustomed to the rituals of their various holidays and festivals that it was impossible to do away with them entirely. Therefore, in the year 496 A. D., Pope Galasius of Rome chose a different patron as a sort of substitute for the observance of the day. The Lupercalia had come on February 15th. At the same time of the year, February 14th to be exact, more than two hundred years before, a Bishop by the name of Valentine had been executed on Palestine Hill where once had stood the altar to Pan, and so the Christian Church decided that St. Valentine should be honored on this day, in place of the Lupercalia festival of the 15th. St. Valentine's Day then took on the old, old customs of the Lupercalia of Ancient Rome, many of which it still retains.

There is very little known of the life of the patron Saint of February 14th, Bishop Valentine. Some historians have claimed that he has been confused with another St. Valentine, who lived during Emperor Claudius' time and was imprisoned for marrying couples secretly when the Emperor, on some pretext, had forbidden the marriages to take place. The best authorities, however, place our St. Valentine as being the churchman who was beaten and beheaded on

February 14, 269 A. D., because he had cured his jail-
keeper's daughter of blindness. He is buried in the church
of St. Praxedes at Rome where a gate was named for him,
Porto Valentini. This gate was later named the *Porta del
Popolo.*

The author Brand, in his "Popular Antiquities," claims
that St. Valentine's Day has been observed since 1446. In
literature the holiday is mentioned by Chaucer and Shakespeare. It was Ophelia in Shakespeare's Hamlet who sang:

> *Good morrow! 'tis St. Valentine's Day*
> *All in the morning betime,*
> *And I a maid at your window,*
> *To be your Valentine!*

The oldest custom of the day, in England and Scotland,
because it had come down from the Lupercalia, was that of
drawing names from an urn. But this practice has long since
died out. In Norwich, England, St. Valentine's Day used to
be a day for giving gifts. These were presented in the
manner of May baskets, and were left at the doorstep of
the recipient. So general was the custom at one time, that
it was said the noise of the knockers of people leaving their
baskets made a horrible din. In the town of Norfolk it was
the custom for children to catch each other for valentines.
They would quote, " good morrow, Valentine " and if they

could repeat this before they were spoken to, they were rewarded with a small gift, while in Oxfordshire the boys and girls collected pennies by singing along the streets these words:

> *Good morning to you, Valentine,*
> *Curl your locks as I do mine,*
> *Two before and three behind,*
> *Good morrow to you, Valentine.*

In Derbyshire the girls used to look through the keyhole early on the morning of St. Valentine's Day and " if they saw only a single object or person they would remain unmarried all that year. If they saw, however, two or more objects or persons, they would be sure to have a sweetheart, and that in no distant time; but if fortune so favored them that by chance they saw a cock and a hen, they might be certain of being married before the year was out." In this place also there was the belief that if a maid would run around the church twelve times at midnight repeating:

> *I sow hempseed, hempseed I sow,*
> *He that loves me best come after me now,*

she would be sure to see her future husband!

A very old saying claimed that if snowdrops were brought into the house before St. Valentine's Day the single women of that house would remain unmarried all year! Other superstitions along this line are evident in the following extract from a young lady's diary for 1754:

" Last Friday was Valentine's Day and the night before I got five bay-leaves, and pinned four of them to the four corners of my pillow, and the fifth to the middle; and then if I dreamt of my sweetheart, we should be married before the year is out. But to make it sure, I boiled an egg hard and took out the yolk, and filled it with salt; and when I went to bed ate it, shell and all, without speaking or drinking after it. We also wrote our lovers' names upon bits of paper, and rolled them up in clay, and put them into water; and the first that rose up was to be our valentine."

To the young people of today a state of uncertainty about the future would be preferable to such drastic measures as that described!

There has always been a superstition among rural people that the birds selected their mates on St. Valentine's Day.

It is still the custom in England for children to go about on Valentine's Eve singing for pennies, apples, or oranges. They have different songs in various localities. Of these one song goes like this:

Good morrow, Valentine,
A piece of bacon, and a piece of cheese
And a bottle of wine.

> *If you've got a penny in your pocket*
> *Slip it into mine.*
> *We used to come at eight o'clock*
> *And now we come at nine.*

In some sections of England it is customary to eat a certain kind of bun made with caraway seeds or currants. At Rutland these are called shittles; in some places they contain plums and are known as plum shittles. In Rutland these buns have been given to the boys and girls of the town on St. Valentine's Day for hundreds of years.

Young people in Denmark exchange valentines in a unique form. These are pressed snowdrops, and with the dried flower they send a greeting which they have composed themselves, in rhyme. These *gaekkebrev* are a much more personal form of valentine than the commercial type.

The Sicilians hold a happy festival on February 14th. It is said that a young girl in Sicily will stand at her window for a half hour before the sun rises on the morning of St. Valentine's Day, and if she sees no one pass she will have to remain unmarried that year. But if a man should happen to come within sight of her watching eyes, it means that either he or someone closely resembling him will become her husband, and that within the year!

February 22

WASHINGTON'S BIRTHDAY

America has furnished to the world the character of Washington. And if our American institutions had done nothing else, that alone would have entitled them to the respect of mankind.
—Daniel Webster.

To know the history of our country is to know Washington. He stands justly with the greatest statesmen the world has ever known. Washington was born February 11, 1732, according to the Old Style calendar then still in use. The New Style calendar adoption changed the date to February 22d, and that date is now a legal holiday in all of the States and Possessions of the United States.

It is unusual for a famous person to have his birthday celebrated before his death, but that happened to George

Washington. The first celebration of Washington's Birthday took place in Newport, Rhode Island, on February 11, 1781, eighteen years before his death. The day was made a holiday, with French troops parading the streets and cannons booming their salutes in honor of the commanding General, beloved hero of a new nation. For several years February 11th was observed as Washington's Birthday, then in 1790 New York and Richmond began to celebrate the new date, February 22d. It is interesting to note that for a number of years the day was observed in some cities on the eleventh, in others on the twenty-second.

Washington's adopted daughter, Nellie Custis, was married on what proved to be his last birthday, February 22, 1799. The combined wedding and birthday must have been a memorable day at Mount Vernon. It is not hard to imagine the beautiful home of George and Martha Washington as it must have been on that occasion, with many guests thronging the well-furnished rooms, hundreds of candles throwing a soft light over the scene, and huge fires blazing in the fireplaces to keep out the chill winter winds which blew up from the Potomac. Noted for its true Southern hospitality, Mount Vernon was a regal home. Today it is one of the show-places of America.

Washington died that same year, on December 14th. Although a vault was erected under the dome of the

Capitol for his last resting-place, his body was interred in the Mount Vernon Tomb. Washington's Tomb is said to be the most visited shrine in the United States, a half million persons annually paying tribute to the grave of our country's first president.

There are innumerable memorials to Washington in the United States; the most famous, of course, is Washington, D. C. The State of Washington and at least nine cities or towns have been named for him, as have seven colleges. The Washington Monument, a beautiful white marble shaft of more than 555 feet in height, was begun in 1848 and completed in 1884. Forty years after it was started it was opened to the public, and since then millions of people have ascended this unusual structure and looked down upon the city of gleaming white buildings below.

Besides Mount Vernon, Washington's birthplace at Wakefield, Virginia (recently restored), and his boyhood home have also been made into shrines. The latter is on the Rappahannock River near Fredericksburg, Virginia. George Washington spent his boyhood years there from the age of seven until fifteen. Still another memorial is the De Wint House at Tappan, New York, near the George Washington Bridge, this house having been General Washington's headquarters on several occasions during the Revolutionary War.

As stated before, Washington's Birthday is a legal holiday throughout the nation, and all the public schools observe the day with appropriate programs. Perhaps the most unique celebration of the day is that in Biddeford and Saco, Maine—where tar-tub fires have been burned annually for more than 170 years. This strange custom originated at the close of the Revolution through Squire Samuel Pierson, one of Washington's private clerks in the war. His birthday was the same as Washington's, and he probably wanted to celebrate the occasion in some unusual way. Tubs filled with tar were set on fire and pulled through the town amid much shouting and cheering. Though the custom earned the name of tar-tub fires, they have gradually evolved into many individual barrel bonfires.

The greatest celebration of Washington's Birthday took place in 1932, the Bi-Centennial Year. The year's observance opened formally at midnight on New Year's Eve by the striking of a grandfather clock that had belonged to Washington's mother, Mary Ball Washington, which was heard by radio from coast to coast. Thus began a memorable year's celebration, for the 200th anniversary of the birth of Washington was observed throughout the United States and its possessions, as well as in 259 cities in eighty-one countries of the world. The formal celebration lasted from February 21st until Thanksgiving Day, with special emphasis on holidays like Memorial Day, Flag Day, Independence Day and Thanksgiving. New York City, for instance, started the Bi-Centennial there on February 21st with parades, meetings and special addresses, radio programs and plays, exhibits and flag displays. In Washington, the anniversary was opened on the same day by President Hoover's speech to Congress on George Washington, followed by the singing of "America" by twelve thousand persons.

Never had there been such a well-planned celebration of a national hero in any land. As Director of the United States George Washington Bi-Centennial Commission, Mr. Sol Bloom made it possible for every city and community, every school and organization in the country to take part. The Commission had been created by Congress in 1924 and no stone was left unturned, no detail neglected to make the anniversary year a success. The event also was observed with sincerity in Italy, France, Germany, Japan, Poland, Australia, England, Cuba and India. The Polish Government, in connection with the Bi-Centennial, presented to President Hoover an elaborately engraved stamp. Fitted within a red leather binding, it contained three pictures: that of George Washington in the center, with the Polish heroes of the American Revolution, Pulaski and Kosciusko, on either side.

A series of twelve special stamps issued by the United

States Post Office commemorated the Bi-Centennial year. Each of the twelve stamps showed Washington as he has been painted or sculptured by a famous artist.

Among some of the outstanding achievements of the Bi-Centennial are the following:

Fourteen large murals painted by American artists to hang in the National Museum.

The collection and publication of Washington's entire writings.

Ten million trees planted in his honor.

A spectacular pageant at the foot of the Washington Monument lasting for three days, in which 10,000 persons participated.

Contests in prose essays and verse on Washington conducted by schools all over the United States.

Probably the most far-reaching result of the Bi-Centennial was its educational effect. An intensive study of the life of Washington was made by millions of school children. His biographies were read and his principles and the effect of those principles on the making of a nation were studied. Surely his high ideals of government, his courage as a soldier, his patience as a commander, and his devotion to his country could not help but create hero-worship in the hearts of many. To one man who took the presidency seventy-two years later, George Washington was a model after whom much of his own life was molded. Although the lives of Washington and Lincoln were materially different, their ideals and aspirations were in many ways similar. Washington, being a man of great wealth, was accustomed to slavery, but he did not accept it in his own mind as being right. In a speech many years after Washington's death, President McKinley discussed the first President's views on slavery: "Washington's views on slavery were characterized by a high sense of justice and an exalted conscience. He was the owner of slaves by inheritance, all his interests were affected by slavery, yet he was opposed to it, and in his will he provided for the liberation of his slaves. He set the example for emancipation. He hoped for, prayed for, and was willing to vote for what Lincoln afterward accomplished."

When George Washington was elected president of the United States in New York City, in 1789, travel was so difficult that it took him seventeen days to make the journey from Virginia to New York for his inauguration. But what a unique and enviable position his was! The office he was to fill was highest in the land. He was to head a new nation that had been settled and colonized by brave, hardy groups of men and women and established by their valorous descendants. Washington, as he took the oath of office, must have realized the solemnity of the moment. After the inauguration he made a prayer for the new country for which he had fought and over which he was to preside. He had been a great soldier, so was he to be a great President.

ST. PATRICK'S DAY

St. Patrick belongs to Ireland. Sure, 'n' all the Saints in Heaven must know that that's a fact! Ireland—St. Patrick—the shamrock! The three seem so closely related that it is, in itself, reminiscent of that three-leafed symbol, the shamrock. But, though Patrick is Ireland's patron saint, beloved by every true son of Erin, he was not a native Irishman for he was not born on Irish soil. Considering that his is one of the best-loved names in history, the actual facts of St. Patrick's life are surprisingly vague, and most of the stories that have survived concerning him are flavored with legend. His biographers usually disagree on all the main facts of his life—the date and place of his birth and death, for instance; but we are able, in spite of their disagreements, to piece together with some accuracy a fairly coherent account of St. Patrick's exciting life.

He was born about 387 A. D. in a small Roman town in what is now probably Wales. There is a wide difference of opinion concerning the country of his birth, that honor having been claimed by England, Scotland and France as well as by Wales. He was born of a patrician family by the name of Sucat, and his father was a member of the magistracy of the town. The boy was named Maewyn; it was not until many years later that he was given the name of Patricius. From the time of his boyhood, he seemed predestined for adventure and achievement. The adventure began when the boy, at the age of sixteen, was captured by pirates and sold into slavery. He soon found himself in a strange land, in the county of Antrim in Ireland. It was a life spent entirely out in the open for, a slave, he was put to work as a swineherd. It is thought that the six years spent in the wild new country furnished him with the inspiration that influenced the whole course of his life. It is pretty certain that it was at this time he determined to spend his life in an effort to free the people of that country from paganism. From his own " Confessions " which have been translated from the Latin, Patrick tells how, after six years of service, he saw a vision and heard a voice saying: " Behold, a ship is ready for thee," and how he finally managed to escape from serfdom, then secured passage on a boat as in his vision, finally reaching his own home.

Maewyn was then a young man of twenty-two years. With his mind firmly fixed on his purpose he set out to receive the training he needed. He spent four years at Tours, France, in study. But the serious young man was again halted in his life work when he was captured a second time and sent into slavery. From his "Confessions" we learn that it was during this time that he again heard the voices of many people coming from the dark mysterious forests of Ireland, bidding him to help them.

Patrick was enslaved only two months this time. After his return to his studies, by degrees he became priest, bishop, and statesman. Then in the year 431 A. D., after having received the ecclesiastical name of Patricius from Pope Celestine, he was at last sent by the Pope to Ireland, according to his wishes, to free the people from paganism and convert them to Christianity. It is believed that St. Patrick landed at Wicklow Head in the Spring of 432 A. D. One historian tells of this landing.

"When St. Patrick landed near Wicklow, the inhabitants were ready to stone him for attempting an innovation in the religion of their ancestors. He requested to be heard, and explained unto them that God is an omnipotent sacred Spirit, who created Heaven and Earth, and that the Trinity is contained in the Unity; but they were reluctant to give credit to his words. St. Patrick, therefore, plucked a trefoil (shamrock) from the ground, and expostulated with the Hibernians: 'Is it not as possible for the Father, Son, and Holy Ghost, as for these three leaves to grow upon a single stalk? ' Then the Irish were immediately convinced of their error, and were solemnly baptized by St. Patrick."

It is doubtful, however, whether St. Patrick was so easily able to convince his listeners. It is said that he was forced back to his ship after his first landing at Wicklow, and had to land farther along at Lecale. But that Patrick's persistence was successful is too well known for dispute. His success was so overwhelming in achievement in this wilderness, that he was able to establish 365 churches and as many schools and one or two colleges, consecrate at least two bishops, baptize approximately 120,000 persons, and Christianize the population of a country whose history up to that time had been one of complete paganism. Patrick was a man whose fearlessness was more than a match for the Druids in spite of their previous undisputed hold on the people. The pagan priests were of course his worst enemies, especially the *Druadh*. They were the magicians or physicians among the people, steeped in the art of their mysterious and terrible cult, ages old. The Irish had for so long believed in the existence of spirits, phantoms, and gods who were all a power of evil that it was the only thing they could understand. St. Patrick must have been aware of this when he chose trefoil to illustrate to them in an understandable manner the Trinity of the Christian God. For the trefoil was to the Druids not just an ordinary clover. It had been assigned a magic power by the *Druadh*, and was thought of by the people as being a symbol of magic.

All of the stories that have come down to us through the ages concerning St. Patrick have an air of mystery and color about them. It is said that wherever he went Patrick was preceded by a drummer, and that the mysterious beat of the drum through the forests would announce to all who heard it that the great foreign Bishop was approaching. The strange and unusual was expected of him, and Patrick had an amazing way of reaching these uncivilized people through their imaginations.

The life of St. Patrick after an almost unbelievable career came to an end on March 17th in the district of Saul, in the year 465, it is believed. When the news of his death reached the people they came flocking to his funeral by the thousands. There were so many torches and candles carried in the procession that it was said to be light as day at that place; and from that, probably, has sprung the story that during the days between his death and burial the sun never went down at all. Patrick was buried at Downpatrick in

Ireland, and later two other saints were placed beside him. According to a monk who lived many years ago, " On the hill of Down, buried in one tomb, were Bridget and Patricius, with Columba the Pious."

The best known story of St. Patrick is that which tells how he rid the land of Ireland of snakes. In Chambers' " Book of Days " we read: " The greatest of St. Patrick's miracles was that of driving the venomous reptiles out of Ireland, and rendering the Irish soil, forever after, so obnoxious to the serpent race that they instantaneously die on touching it."

These lines are quoted by Chambers from a poet in regard to another miraculous story of the saint:

Saint Patrick, as in legends told,
The morning being very cold,
In order to assuage the weather,
Collected bits of ice together;
Then gently breathed upon the pyre,
When every fragment blazed on fire.

He is attributed with having raised several people from the dead, one of them having been his own father.

It is said that St. Patrick's Day is always clear because the saint had petitioned it so! Even today there is the belief that every alternate day after March 17th will be bright and sunshiny, and in Ireland and wherever the Irish live there is the popular belief that after St. Patrick's Day it is time to plant the garden.

Since Patrick is Ireland's patron saint, March 17th, commemorating the day of his death, is the most important day of the calendar in that country. For hundreds of years it has been celebrated with great joy and the gayest of ceremonies. Parades and speeches are the order of the day, after High Mass. The evenings are spent with music and dancing and general hilarity. The people try in every way to do as the old ballad bids them: " Saint Patrick's Day, we'll all be very gay."

It used to be the custom for the wealthy people of Ireland to brew ale along in February and keep it till St. Patrick's Day when pickled salmon and oaten bread were eaten with it. The innkeepers would give a " Patrick's Pot "—a quantity of ale or whisky—to everybody, free! To " drown the shamrock " with a Patrick's Pot was an unvariable custom of every St. Patrick's evening. Over the Patrick's Pot the jovial company wished each other health and riches, including " long leases and low rents."

" Drowning the shamrock " was done by the devotee of St. Patrick dipping the shamrock in his glass of liquor then touching it with the shamrock in his hatband. The shamrock or trefoil (sometimes called hop-clover) grows in great abundance in Ireland and is often used there as a watercress. It is still believed by many to have curative powers, this belief having come down from the ancient Druids and been strengthened, probably, by the importance it assumed through St. Patrick's connection with it. As the national emblem of Ireland, the shamrock forms a part of the British coat-of-arms. In the great British emblem, the rose is for England, the thistle for Scotland, and the shamrock for Ireland.

Symbols seem to have great significance among the Irish. One writer in describing the observance of St. Patrick's Day describes the *croiseog* worn in that country. He says: " On this day every child throughout Ireland, excepting Connemara and some of the northern districts, is expected to wear upon the left breast a small disk intersected by crosses upon the surface and known as *croiseog* or ' favor.' In Connemara the *croiseog* is worn only by the women. They are of various designs and colors, but the general pattern is everywhere the same. ... . In Clare and Connemara there is usually but one cross, drawn upon the surface of the disk with the blood of the wearer, the blood being obtained by pricking the finger. The green is usually procured from grass and the yellow from the yolk of an egg."

Today in Ireland as in years gone by there can be seen on St. Patrick's Day picturesque old women selling the three-leafed trefoil. " Buy my shamrock, green shamrock! " they call to passers-by. On this day it is customary for the rich to give to the poor. In Dublin the very elite of the upper classes are invited to an impressive ball at Dublin Castle. It is held in a large ballroom known as St. Patrick's Hall which has been the scene of this annual social function for many years. The ball is attended each year now by the President of the Irish Free State.

There is always a big parade in Dublin as well as a true Irish dance festival. One great difference between the old time St. Patrick's Day celebrations and those of today is that now on March 17th there is little or no " drowning of the shamrock," and instead of the old green flag of tradition with the proverbial harp, there is a new flag that floats over the country—green, orange and white, the flag of the free country of Eire! To the freedom-loving people of the country of St. Patrick, it is the most beautiful in all the world. If it had not been for St. Patrick and his perseverance, it might not wave today.

St. Patrick's Day has been observed in New York City since 1762. The celebrations staged by the Irish in the cities of New York, Chicago, San Francisco, and Boston exceed those of good old Dublin. St. Patrick's Cathedral is always the focal point of interest in the spectacular parades in New York. In 1934 I saw a typical New York " St. Pat's " Parade.

Twenty thousand marchers made their way down Fifth Avenue in the early spring sunshine to the tunes of numerous bands. "When Irish Eyes are Smiling," "Wearing of the Green," etc., met with hearty cheers from the throng of half a million spectators. The young lads of the parochial schools, whose fife and drum corps added to the music of the procession, lent color to the scene with their brilliant red capes. Thousands of parading children were dressed appropriately in green, and the kilts of the pipers were green in honor of the Emerald Isle. Shamrocks and green flags and green hats were in evidence on almost every individual who watched the parade.

In the city of Rome, St. Patrick's Day takes on a different kind of observance. In the 365 churches there, the day is celebrated with much pomp and ceremony in a truly commemorative manner. As this church service seems to be the only observance of its kind in St. Patrick's honor, perhaps it is the sort the good saint would have liked best of all,—remembering the Church for which he stood, and preserving his Day as a Saint Day.

March or April

EASTER

Easter is the time of year for chocolate bunnies and eggs and hot cross buns. It seems natural enough for us to eat these at the accustomed time, but do we ever stop to think why? Why should we have bunnies, of all things, at Easter? There *is* a reason.

The bunny is really a hare and, according to legends of far-off Egypt, the hare is a symbol of the moon. Everyone knows that the date of Easter is determined by the moon. In the year 325 A. D. Constantine had the uncertain date of this holy day settled for all time by taking the matter before the Council of Nicea. The worthy and wise ones of the Council decided that Easter should fall upon *the first Sunday*

after the first full moon after the twenty-first day of March!
And so the hare, or bunny, has come into prominence
because of the moon's importance in reckoning Easter.

As for Easter eggs! They are so closely bound up with
Easter that it would be like taking the Christmas tree away
from a Christmas celebration to eliminate eggs from an
Easter festival. Wherever this holiday is observed, eggs play
some part in the celebration. The egg is the symbol of new
life and that, probably, is the reason they have come to
hold so much significance at the commemoration of the
Resurrection. For hundreds of years dyed eggs have been
exchanged as a token of peace at Easter. In fact, we can
trace the custom of egg-giving back to the ancient Egyptians,
long before the time of Christ. The custom was prevalent
among the ancient Hebrews also, for the Paschal egg held
an important place at the festive board of the Passover.

In the eighteenth century, egg-races were the main event
at the Easter fêtes in certain parts of France. The winner
of the race was given a hogshead of cider as a prize. Egg-
games and egg-races have not lost their popularity even
today. In our own national capital at Washington every
year, on Easter Monday, there is the famous egg-rolling contest for children on the White House lawn. In England,
especially in the northern shires, egg-rolling is an annual
event. Eggs are saved all through Holy Week for the sport

on Easter Day. Children of Bohemia and Germany also like to roll eggs at Easter time. The Germans often roll the eggs on tracks made of sticks; the sport starts at midnight and lasts until near dawn on Easter morning.

In Ireland at dawn on Easter Day eggs are eaten to break the Fast of Lent, while eggs in Scotland are used by the boys and girls for a game of ball! In the Tyrol, children carry baskets and torches and sing Easter carols as they travel through the valley from farmhouse to farmhouse on Easter Eve. At each place they are given bright colored eggs to put into their baskets, the farmers' wives having vied with each other in coloring and decorating them, even printing mottoes on their hard shells. The children of Mesopotamia gather all the eggs they can during the forty days of Lent, selling them at Eastertide in the market places. The boys and girls of many of our rural sections here in America save eggs during Lent, too, coloring them for Easter baskets, and children in Belgium make nests of hay and hide them in the grass on the day before Easter, knowing full well that Easter morning will show them overflowing with eggs—both dyed ones and those made of chocolate.

In Italy, eggs take on a more reverential rôle. They are carried to church by the hundreds and blessed by the priests. Then they are taken home and given the center of the table as the main dish at the Easter Feast. Everything on the table is arranged around the eggs—the food, the best silver and flowers. Sometimes they number as many as two hundred, all colored in the most brilliant and arresting hues of red, blue, purple and gold. Visitors to the house during Easter Week must not refuse this sacred food of the Resurrection.

The people of the Ukraine, according to custom, like to rub the dyed red eggs against their cheeks to make them glow, adding to their look of happiness at the Easter Feast. In Russia, before the Soviet Union changed the custom, rich and poor alike exchanged dyed eggs at Easter time with the greeting, " Jesus Christ is risen! " Here, too, the eggs had been blessed at the church where, early on Easter morning, it was customary for the priests to bless the food which the people had piled in great colorful heaps—hard bright eggs and pyramids of curds lavishly embellished.

> *One-a-penny buns,*
> *Two-a-penny buns,*
> *One-a-penny, two-a-penny,*
> *Hot cross buns!*

So sings the bun peddler in England! Nowhere in the world are hot cross buns sold or eaten except during Lent. They are, most especially, an item of Friday fare. With the sign of the cross made in their delicious top crusts, they have become emblematic of that Friday many hundreds of years ago on which Christ died on the Cross. In olden times the eating of hot cross buns was said to protect the house from fire for the ensuing year. Some even believed that, ground up, the crumbs of the buns could be added to water and used for medicinal purposes the year round. From *Poor Robin's Almanack* we are told:

> *Good Friday comes this month, the old woman runs*
> *With one- or two-a-penny hot cross buns,*
> *Whose virtue is, if you believe what's said,*
> *They'll not grow mouldy like the common bread.*

To-day in France on Shrove Tuesday and Ash Wednesday it is customary to eat pancakes; this practice also is observed in those parts of America where French people have settled. In old Russia, cakes fried in butter and called *blinnies* were eaten by everyone the week preceding Lent. And in Switzerland it was *Fastnacht* cake, made with caraway seeds. Strangely enough, this custom of eating buns, pancakes and the like at the Easter season emanated from the pagan practice of eating cakes in honor of the goddess Eostre, many centuries ago.

Eostre was the Anglo-Saxon name for the Teutonic goddess of Spring, Ostera. There is no doubt but what the fair goddess lent considerable influence to the early Christians in the naming of Easter. The pagan observance of the awakening of Earth from her long winter's sleep quite naturally evolved into the significance as we know it now of the Awakening or Resurrection of our Lord from three days' sleep in the tomb. This similarity of names, Eostre and Easter, suggests that our holiest of all holidays has derived its name from a pagan festival.

Many of the Easter customs among people of foreign lands would seem strange indeed to us who are not accustomed to them, but to those who observe them they are an inherited element in their lives. Dancing in Spain on Easter Day, for instance, so different from our own observance of the holy day, is truly a national characteristic of the music-loving Spaniards. Ukrainian girls in their country dance the traditional *hahilki,* accompanied by the happy voices of the dancers raised in the merry *hahilki* songs. All over Ireland, too, there is dancing on Easter Sunday. Over the entire countryside old and young alike compete for a prize cake with their dancing, and long hours of fun and excitement prevail before the winning couple " takes the cake."

Among the Tyrolese farmers there is apt to be dismay when Shrove Tuesday comes around. With the same spirit of mischief that invades our own rural districts on Hallowe'en, on Shrove Tuesday the prank-loving boys of that place lead the farmer's cow into his kitchen-garden, hide his gate, and hoist his cart and wheelbarrow to the roof of his house!

During Lent in Hungary social life for adults is at a standstill, but for the young people there is a unique game played with fire called *sajbozas*. A combination of ritual and sport, it is played in an open field or pasture in the evening on the first Sunday of Lent. The girls set fire to a small hut of timber that has been built beforehand. From this, after the blaze has somewhat subsided, the boys heat *sajbo* rings in the hot flames. With a clever twist of a stick they send the red-hot rings flying through the darkness, with an effect not unlike the fireworks of our Fourth of July.

In Suffolk, England, there used to be a quaint and unusual custom of choosing twelve old women of the village to play ball on Easter Monday, the ball-game coming to an end at sunset. The significance of this custom died out long before its observance did. Another old English custom was " lifting." This strange byplay took place on the two days following Easter. On Easter Monday the men carried a silk-lined chair, adorned with flowers and streamers, merrily through the streets of the village in search of fair damsels! Having met one, she was made to sit in the chair and was then lifted high in the air amid shouts of laughter and shrieks from the fair victim. There was only one means of escaping her captors, and that was to pay a forfeit, often a kiss. On the next day the positions were reversed; the chairs were carried by the women and the men were the victims!

" Clipping the church " was once popular in England at Easter. Hosts of children all dressed in their best for the occasion stood around the church with their backs to the building. Joining hands they formed a complete circle with the church or small chapel in the center of the ring. Each church in the village was " clipped " with serious ceremony.

Until the time of James II, it was customary on Maundy Thursday for the sovereign of England to wash the feet of at least twelve paupers, representing the act of Jesus washing the feet of the twelve disciples at the Last Supper on the day before Good Friday. In history we read of this ritual being performed by good Queen Bess at the age of thirty-nine when she washed the feet of thirty-nine paupers. Maundy Thursday plays an important part in the ceremonies of Holy Week in the Catholic Church. Among the Volhynian Ukrainians on that day many people bathe in the river for it is believed at that time to have curative powers. At night they have supper, at which special dishes are eaten, commemorating the Last Supper. Ukrainians observe the Easter season for two weeks, beginning with Willow Sunday (our Palm Sunday). The first week is observed with reverence, the second is devoted to social activity. Usually the peasants go back to their labors on the Thursday after Easter, but all the evenings are spent in visiting, dancing and card-playing. In fact the festive evenings continue until Ascension Day. These people through all the political strife they have known have clung tenaciously to the customs that have been so endeared to them down through the ages. Even in America they keep up the traditions that are so much a part of themselves, and it has been my privilege to eat the *paska* and other Ukrainian dishes in the home of friends that had been blessed at midnight Mass the night before.

There is a peculiar ceremony that takes place in Greece on Good Friday. A wooden effigy of Jesus, followed by a procession of people, is carried through the streets with great ceremony and then given burial. This funeral of course is to express sorrow over Jesus' death on the Cross. In Mexico effigies of Judas Iscariot, the disciple who betrayed Jesus, are severely dealt with at high noon on Holy Saturday. Thousands of Judas Iscariots, of all sizes and shapes and of hideous caricature, are hanged, beaten, burned, and otherwise punished by the hot-blooded Mexicans who throng the streets for the occasion.

The French people, with their love for fêtes and their enthusiasm over all holidays, celebrate Easter with proper religious dignity, observing Lent in the manner of the

Roman Catholic Church. But the forty days of Lent are preceded by carnivals all over France, the most famous of which is held on Shrove Tuesday. In Paris there is a grand carnival on Mid-Lent Sunday at which beauty queens are chosen to preside, and a fatted ox is the main feature of the colorful procession that winds its way through the famous streets of Paris. Because of the fact that in years gone by Easter was also the first of the new year, one still occasionally hears the greeting " Happy New Year! " which falls strangely upon the ear at this time.

It seems strange for us to think of Easter as being any different in this country than it is today, but it has been only in the past fifty years that the churches of all denominations have observed Easter with any marked ceremony. At first it was only the Catholic churches that kept it. Thus Virginia and Louisiana, because they were settled by Catholics, were the first states to observe Easter as a church festival, and the New England States were the last to acknowledge it as a holiday.

Sunrise services at dawn on Easter Day have become an established feature of an American Easter. One of the first places in the United States to have held Easter sunrise services was Bethlehem, Pennsylvania. About three o'clock on Easter morning the Moravian Trombone Choir sends a message through the still clear air to the people of the town

from the steeple of the church, calling them to the service.
Thousands of men, women and children throng into the old
Moravian Burying Ground beyond the church to await the
dawn of Easter Day. " Christ is risen! " The voices sing the
message to the accompaniment of the trombones as the sun
appears over the surrounding purple hills. The dawn of
another Easter is greeted with new hope by these people
whose ancestors established the new Bethlehem and the
Moravian Church in America.

Even in far-off Hawaii this custom has been wholeheartedly adopted. In Honolulu every year there is a glorious
Easter sunrise service held at the Punchbowl, a volcanic
crater which stands, passive now, overlooking the city.

It would take too long to tell of the beautiful and solemn
religious services in the great churches and cathedrals over
all the Christian world,—of the magnificence of Easter at
St. Peter's Cathedral in Rome, or of the pilgrimages to
Jerusalem, the Holy City. In America, with well-trained
choirs in every town and city rendering their Stabat Maters
and Bach Masses and inspiring hymns of the Resurrection,
and millions of people filling the churches to overflowing
on Easter Sunday, this is without doubt the holiest of all
our holidays. The religious observance of Easter is surely
the most significant " custom " of all, for it commemorates
that very first Easter more than nineteen hundred years

ago when the angel of the Lord spoke from a sepulchre garden:

" He is not here: for he is risen."

On this day are people sent ...on purpose for pure merriment

April 1

APRIL FOOLS' DAY

April First can hardly be called a holiday, but it is one of those days of the calendar which refuse to be relegated to the place of just an ordinary day. After at least three hundred years of being the one day in the year's 365 when it is permissible to " befool " people, the custom still persists. Though All Fools' Day is in no way recognized by governments, nor encouraged by our public schools, and is seldom mentioned by writers and certainly never praised in song or verse, it continues to hold its own in the minds of the people. On this day, from the time we get up in the morning until we go to bed, we can expect to fall prey to an April Fool joke.

Back in 1760 these lines were written in *Poor Robin's Almanack:*

The first of April, some do say,
Is set apart for All Fools' Day;
But why the people call it so
Nor I, nor they themselves, do know.
But on this day are people sent
On purpose for pure merriment.

" Nor I, nor they themselves, do know " is as true today as it was then! The origin of this day is vague, the reasons for its observance having long been lost while its customs still prevail. There are evidences of All Fools' Day being observed in England as early as the seventeenth century; it is thought to have been copied by the English from the French. Although there are other conjectures concerning its origin, the following seems to be the one most accepted by historians.

From time immemorial the vernal equinox has been observed by all classes of people. This occurs around March 21st. Up until the time of the Gregorian Calendar, adopted in the sixteenth century, March 21st was also the beginning of the New Year! In those days the New Year ushered in a whole week of celebrations, and the last or eighth day of the festivities was devoted to the exchange of gifts. In the year 1564 Pope Gregory introduced a new calendar which France was the first country to adopt. March 21st was no longer the beginning of the New Year, and April first was no longer the most important day in the combined New Year and Vernal Equinox celebrations. But in those days news traveled very slowly, and consequently they continued to celebrate April first as the last glorious day of the New Year celebrations. Greetings were exchanged, and gifts given as before. But these people who still clung to the old calendar, either through ignorance or just through die-hard custom, soon became known as April Fools. And thus it was that in France the first day of April came gradually to develop into a day of fooling and being fooled! The custom then spread into England and beyond.

The most popular form of fooling has always been to send the victim of the jest on some fruitless errand. Quoting again from *Poor Robin's Almanack:*

> . . . *In sending fools to get intelligence*
> *One seeks hen's teeth in farthest part of the town;*
> *Another pigeon's milk; a third a gown*
> *From strolling cobbler's stall, left there by chance;*
> *Thus lead the giddy tribe a merry dance.*
> *And to reward them for their harmless toil,*
> *The cobbler 'noints their limbs with stirrup oil.*
> *Thus by contrivers' inadvertent jest,*
> *One fool exposed makes pastime for the rest.*

In certain parts of England the time for playing April Fool jokes is limited to the morning hours. If anyone should forget this rule and play a joke after the noon hour, the fooler becomes the fool! In Hampshire they say: " April Fool's gone past; You're the biggest fool at last." Many are the witless errands the poor unsuspecting April noddie is sent upon. The person who so far forgets his dates as to " fall " for the jests of the first of April has earned many nicknames. In England besides being a noddie, he is called a gawby, a gobby, or an April gob! In Scotland he is called an April Gowk, and there a gowk is a cuckoo! When the Scotch send a victim on a foolish errand they say he is hunting the Gowk.

The French are apt to send the April fish for some " sweet vinegar " or " a stick with only one end " ! In France the person fooled on April first is called an April fish, *un poisson d'Avril.* This expression seems very appropriate

since he " bites " on the joke and is " caught." But it is likely the *fish* has been borrowed from the sign of the zodiac, *Pisces.*

In Provence on this day everybody eats peas which are peculiar to that place called *pois chiches*. In years gone by April Fool victims were sent to the Convent of Chartreux in Provence to ask for these peas. It seems that because of a vow made previously by the convent fathers, peas were given to all who asked for them.

In Lisbon, Portugal, All Fools' Day is observed on the Sunday and Monday preceding Lent. There the people threw ashes or flour into each other's faces, a most peculiar custom the significance of which is unknown.

In India there is a day corresponding to All Fools' Day, called the Feast of the Huli. A celebration of the Equinox, it is observed on March 31st and is so similar to April Fools' Day that it seems more than likely that they have had the same origin. Brand in his " Popular Antiquities " tells us: " During the Huli, when mirth and festivity reign among the Hindoos of every class, one subject of diversion is to send people on errands and expeditions that are to end in disappointment, and raise a laugh at the expense of the person sent."

" The Day of Innocent Martyr Saints " is observed in Mexico (December 28th) in a way that is reminiscent of April Fools' Day. There the children have a custom of fooling members of their family, or the neighbors, by borrowing something of value such as small sums of money or some prized possession, and instead of returning it, replacing it with some worthless trinket. The invaluable substitute in this strange custom is accompanied by a note which reminds the victim of the trick and that they never should have lent anything on the *Dia de los Inocentes!*

There is a funny story told by historians about an April Fool joke that was played in London many years ago. Several days before the first of April invitations were sent to many of the city's most prominent persons. They read:

" Tower of London—Admit Bearer and Friend to view annual ceremony of Washing the White Lions on Sunday, April 1, 1860. Admittance only at White Gate."

Many cabs drove around Tower Hill that Sunday morning searching for the White Gate! It was said that those who lived in the vicinity were greatly disturbed with all the noise, and very curious too as to what it was all about.

Another story comes down to us from history. It tells how Francis, Duke of Lorraine, and his wife were being held in captivity at Nantes, France. On the first day of April they disguised themselves as peasants and at an early hour of the morning attempted to pass through the city gates. All went well until the guard, informed of their identity, was told to give word to the sentry that those two were in reality Francis and his wife. But when the guard heard it he shouted with laughter and cried, "April Fool!" The word flew along the lines to the guards there, and all considered it a huge April Fool joke. However, when the Governor heard it he was suspicious. But too late. The Duke and his wife had escaped because of the fact that the day they had chosen for their escape was April first, All Fools' Day.

Date Varies for Different States

ARBOR DAY

Although Arbor Day is a legal holiday in only six states (Arizona, Nebraska, Rhode Island, Texas, Utah, and Wyoming), it is observed in every State in the Union either by proclamation of the Governor of the State or by the Board of Education. The dates of celebration vary, ranging anywhere from January (Louisiana) to December (Georgia), but in most states it is observed in the Spring. A few states celebrate two Arbor Days, and some combine it with Bird Day. In California it is on Luther Burbank's birthday, March 7th.

The first Arbor Day in America was observed in Nebraska

on April 10, 1872. In that year J. Sterling Morton, then a member of the State Board of Agriculture, introduced a resolution at the State Legislature which said: " That Wednesday, the 10th day of April, 1872, be . . . especially set apart and consecrated to tree planting in the State of Nebraska and the State Board of Agriculture hereby name it Arbor Day." At this meeting the resolution was adopted and at the same time prizes were offered, one to an individual and another to the society that planted the greatest number of trees. As a result, more than a million trees were planted in the State on that first Arbor Day. Within the next sixteen years more than 350 million trees were planted, completely transforming a state that was previously a land of vast treeless prairies. Because of this, Nebraska has come to be known as the Tree Planters' State. Later on, Nebraska changed Arbor Day to April 22nd, the birthday of its founder, J. Sterling Morton.

It was almost ten years before any other state became interested in the Arbor Day movement, then Ohio and North Dakota instituted Arbor Day. That year, 1882, Ohio was holding a National Forestry Convention in Cincinnati where the idea was discussed and the advantages pointed out to other states. Two years later at a National Education Association Convention in Connecticut a resolution was introduced to the effect that: " In view of the valuable results of Arbor Day work in the six States where such a day has been observed, alike upon the school and the home, this Association recommends the general observance of Arbor Day for schools in all our States." In 1887 Ontario, Canada, began to observe an Arbor Day on the first Friday in May; the following year New York State took it up, and gradually all the States followed suit.

Other countries as well as our own have days devoted to planting trees. England has a Garland Day at which time children in some sections parade through the streets carrying flowers after they have had a good time weaving them into garlands. In Shropshire on a certain day in May every year there is a huge giant poplar that has been decorated with tiny flags on all of its many branches. This strange custom is to commemorate a wedding that took place in 1786, but why the flags are used on the tree seems to have been forgotten!

Hawaii has had an Arbor Day since 1905. Every year on March 26th Spain celebrates the Fête of the Tree, *Fiesta del Arbol*. This Arbor Day began in 1895 when the youthful King Alfonso planted a pine sapling at a ceremony near Madrid. Germany plants trees on Whitsunday. Palestine observes an Arbor Day annually on February 15th. There is a Floral Festival in Japan on April 8th when the children of Japan, with the priests, offer flowers on the altar of the infant Buddha at the beautiful Flowery Temple.

The Aztec Indians used to have a very nice custom of planting a tree whenever a child was born, a practice that Indians of later tribes continued. An old Colonial custom demanded that a new bride bring a tree from her father's property to plant beside her new home. A feeling of sentiment prompted the young woman to take great care of the new tree to see that it did not die after being transplanted.

Planting trees is of course the purpose of Arbor Day, and many of these are planted as memorials. When the day was first observed in Cincinnati, in 1882, school children of that city planted a grove of trees in Eden Park. It was known as Author's Grove because each tree was named for an author, a statesman, or some other famous person.

One promulgator of Arbor Day was Dr. Birdsey G. Northrup of Connecticut. He not only traveled all over America but in Europe and Asia as well, lecturing and urging people to beautify the world by planting trees. He even offered prizes—a dollar to any child who planted five trees. Civic organizations in cities, towns, and suburbs, as well as the General Federation of Women's Clubs, have urged the same thing and have done a great deal of good in planting shade trees along the streets and highways. Trees also have been planted on the lawns of schools, churches, hospitals and around many public buildings.

The responsibility, however, of planting a tree doesn't end on Arbor Day. Trees must have good care all the year round. In many places Boy Scout Troops are assigned the responsibility of caring for the trees that have been planted on Arbor Day, and in some cases a class in school will assume this duty for the year.

In 1920 a Forest Week was added to the calendar of " Weeks " in the United States; in that year it was from May 23rd to 29th. The next year President Harding changed it to Forest and Protection Week, and four years later it was permanently named American Forest Week. Although observed annually the time of its observance is usually left to the discretion of the individual states.

In 1924 a law was passed enabling landowners to receive forest-tree seeds and plants from the State—one of the biggest aids the non-forested sections of the United States have received.

The estimated combined area of America's 150 national forests amounts to more than 170,000,000 acres. Quoting from a government pamphlet on *Famous Trees:*

" In the United States there is abundant tree growth of the most useful species. The Nation has been quite literally nurtured in a wooden cradle, and its progress has been largely due to the contributions of the forest. The pioneers cut paths through the wilderness—from east to west and from north to south—and the forest harvest has gone into home and community building.

" On all sides there is abundant evidence that forests are essential to civilized man's welfare. The individual tree, however, has an even more intimate part to play in human experience, a part so universal that every country has its famous tree citizens."

The old, old Aztec custom of planting a tree at the birth of a child is as symbolic as it is appropriate, for nothing in all nature seems more endowed with the spirit of life than the tree. As an embryo, it is gently nurtured in the warm pocket of Mother Earth until the seedling has reached maturity. In infancy it reaches its slender green tendrils toward the light of the sun, seeking strength and growth; like a child it shoots up to surprising tallness, growing week by week, month by month, and year by year, to adult stature. Then, in the dignity of maturity, it stands for centuries, a regal monument to the miracle of creation, lending beauty and honor to the world which it graces.

A LIST OF FAMOUS TREES IN AMERICA *

Washington Live Oak. Charleston, S. C. Washington visited Charleston in 1791, and here, so the story goes, was an honored breakfast guest in the beautiful plantation home of the distinguished Pinckney family. He heard the mistress of the household order her gardener to cut down the large oak which obstructed the view from the new portico. Washington, great tree lover that he was, expressed the wish that the tree be spared. It was.

Washington Elm Grandchild. A descendant of the Washington Elm at Cambridge, Mass. (now dead), was planted as a Washington Bi-Centennial tree on the grounds of the State Capitol in Hartford, Conn., on March 31, 1933. The Washington Elm at Cambridge was the tree under which the leader of the American Revolutionary forces assumed command in 1775.

The Lincoln Memorial Hackberry. Decorah, Iowa. It was planted in memory of Abraham Lincoln by John Finn on April 27, 1865, the day that Governor Stone of Iowa set aside as a day of mourning for Lincoln. On that day Finn went into the woods, found a small hackberry tree, and transplanted it to the parking on the street in front of his home. It has grown to be one of the most magnificent trees in Iowa.

Lafayette Sycamore. Near Baltimore Pike, on a hill 200 yards east of the Brandywine Baptist Church, near Chadds Ford,

* Compiled from *Famous Trees,* a publication of the U. S. Department of Agriculture.

Delaware County, Pa., is close to the house occupied by General Lafayette as his headquarters before the Battle of the Brandywine, September 10 and 11, 1777.

Maple. Planted in memory of Juliette Low, founder of the Girl Scouts of America, at Eighteenth Street and New York Avenue, NW, Washington, D. C., by the Girl Scouts of the District of Columbia.

J. Sterling Morton Elm. United States Capitol Grounds, planted in memory of the founder of Arbor Day, by Chief Forester R. Y. Stuart, in 1932. Another is an elm planted by the Nebraska Society at 1214 Sixteenth Street, NW, Washington, D. C., headquarters of the American Tree Association.

Friendship Elm (English elm). Planted by the Duke of Windsor, then Prince of Wales, in Central Park, New York City, in 1920. It is 100 feet from the spot where his grandfather planted an American elm in 1860.

Penn Treaty Elm. At Shackamaxon, Pa., which is now in the Kensington section of Philadelphia, memorable as the place where William Penn concluded his famous treaty with the Indians in 1682. The elm was nearly 300 years old when felled by a storm in 1810. It is perpetuated to the fourth generation, there being seven of its descendants growing in one place, the campus of Haverford College, Haverford, Pa.

Charter Oak. At Hartford, Connecticut, it stood in front of Governor Wyllys' mansion, built in 1638. The charter of the Connecticut Colony, granted by King Charles II in 1662, is supposed to have been hidden in the oak by a patriot when Sir Edmund Andros demanded its surrender in 1687, at the command of King James II. The charter served Connecticut as a constitution from 1662 to 1816 and conveyed to the colony all the land " from the said Narragansett Bay on the east to the South Sea on the west." The tree blew down in a light gale on August 21, 1856. The hole which concealed the charter had been enlarged enough to hold 25 men. Pieces of the wood were made into gavels, picture frames, and even chairs, one of which stands in the senate chamber of the State Capitol.

Council Oak. At Sioux City, Iowa, believed to have been 150 years old when Lewis and Clark saw it on their way to the Pacific coast and there held council with the Indians.

Hendrick Hudson's Tuliptree. Inwood Park, northern end of Manhattan Island, at the mouth of the Harlem River, New York City. Hudson entered this inlet in 1609 and may have met the Indians there. The tree is the only living thing on the island which was there during Hudson's time.

Lombardy Poplar. Planted over 200 years ago at Fort Niagara by the French occupants. It is the sole survivor of a group of these trees planted at the time. This is the only United States Army Post flying three flags—the French, British, and United States.

Louisa May Alcott Elms. In front of the Alcott home and the little grove of pines and spruces just beyond it. The author of " Little Women " once lived under the shade of the elms.

And among the whispering pines Hawthorne walked, thought, and wrote, or conversed with his friend, Thoreau.

Joyce Kilmer Memorial Forest. A 4,000-acre tract of virgin forest near Lake Santeetlah in the Nantahala National Forest, southwestern North Carolina, was dedicated on July 30, 1936, to the poet who wrote " Trees."

Avery Oak. Dedham, Mass., bears the distinction of having been selected as suitable material for the celebrated and much-honored frigate *Old Ironsides.* The amount offered was $70, but the offer was refused because the owner's wife greatly admired the tree.

Mothers of America Tree. European white birch, to memorialize mothers of the Nation; planted east of the United States Capitol Building by the American Forestry Association. It was chosen because of its beauty and dignity.

Road of Remembrance. A thousand elms planted along eight miles of road near Seattle, as the beginning of Memorial Way, dedicated to the soldiers of the State of Washington who died during the World War.

Famous Weeping Birch. Flushing, Long Island, said to be the tree to which is traced the origin of all trees of its kind in the eastern part of the United States.

Black Walnut Tree. Mount Vernon, Virginia, from which walnuts have been taken for planting, by Boy Scouts, all over the country as memorial trees to George Washington.

General Sherman Bigtree. Sequoia National Park, California, has a diameter of 36½ feet or a circumference of nearly 115 feet, a height of 272.4 feet, a volume of 600,120 board feet, and it is between 3,000 and 4,000 years old. Two other immense trees of this type are General Grant Bigtree, of General Grant National Park, and Grizzly Giant Bigtree, in Yosemite National Park, this last estimated at 3,800 years old.

A redwood. Humboldt State Redwood Park, near Dyerville, Humboldt County, California, is said to be " the tallest tree now known." It is 364 feet high. This redwood has been dedicated to the founders of Save-the-Redwoods League and is therefore called the Founders Tree.

A "Sovereign Cypress." In the dense swamp between Sanford and Longwood, Florida, supposed to have been a denizen of this section before Ponce de Leon sought the Fountain of Youth. There is space enough for a roadway to be cut through the trunk. Its estimated age is 3,000 years.

April 14

PAN-AMERICAN DAY

Here is a holiday that belongs to two great continents, the Americas! The United States, Mexico, and the Republics of Central and South America—these are the nations that gave this young holiday its birth, proclaim it annually, and observe it with a spirit of international loyalty. Pan-American Day has sprung from the great need for friendliness and neighborliness, and this makes it one of the most important and significant holidays observed in the Christian world.

A Great Teacher left this Commandment with the world: "Love thy neighbor as thyself." Unfortunately, this Commandment throughout the centuries has meant little or nothing as applied to *nations as neighbors*. One of the definitions of the word neighbor given in the dictionary is:

a fellow man. In ages past with communication so very difficult and with differences in language and custom, it was almost impossible for nations to be neighborly. In those days there was some excuse for unfamiliarity with the rest of the world.

A writer in Buenos Aires in regard to Pan-American Day has said: " To understand each other we need only to know each other." That is true of all nations. In educating the young people of the world to this idea we are taking a definite step toward world peace. For this reason Pan-American Day is very important to all the peoples of the American Republics, and especially to the young people who are learning to know their neighbors.

In the Spring of 1939 the President of the United States, in his annual proclamation that April 14th should be observed as Pan-American Day, called upon the people of the United States, " To observe the Day with appropriate ceremonies thereby giving expression to the spirit of continental solidarity and to the sentiments of cordiality and friendly feeling which the Government and people of the United States entertain toward the people and Governments of the other Republics of the American Continent."

It is still a very young holiday. The year 1940 saw its tenth annual observance. At a meeting of the members of the Pan-American Union on May 7, 1930, the Governing

Board adopted a Resolution in which it was resolved " that the Governments, members of the Pan-American Union, designate April 14th as *Pan-American Day* and that the national flags be displayed on that date." And so it was that April 14th, 1931, was the first Pan-American Day to be observed as a holiday. It was celebrated throughout America. President Hoover asked that the day be observed with appropriate ceremonies in all the schools and that the flag be flown from all public buildings.

This was not, however, the beginning of Pan-Americanism. The first Pan-American Conference of any importance was held in 1826 at Panama when the governments of the Spanish colonies of South America and Central America were represented at a meeting. The United States sent no delegates to that, or to other conferences which followed, until 1889. In that year, when all countries of the American Republics were represented, the Union became organized. This conference lasted for six months! It was held in Washington, D. C., and James G. Blaine, who was then Secretary of State of the United States, was made Chairman of the Union, which called itself The Commercial Bureau of American Republics. In 1910 it was changed to the Pan-American Union. This organization took place on April 14th, 1889, and it was for that reason in 1930 that the date April 14th was chosen as Pan-American Day. From the time of its organization the Pan-American Union was a peace-loving and hopeful body, meeting for discussions of national and international problems concerning themselves and their affairs. This was particularly true of the Latin-American members. In 1901 there was a Pan-American Exposition at Buffalo, New York, to demonstrate this new consciousness of our Southern neighbors. The exposition " to celebrate the progress made in industries, science, and art by American republics during the nineteenth century " was an affair of great and spectacular beauty. Travelers from many lands came to see the " Rainbow City," so-called because of the marvelous display of lights and color.

The year 1937 was an important one in the history of the Union. In that year was held the Pan-American Education Conference in Mexico City, the Inter-American Aviation Conference in Lima, Peru, and the Inter-American Radio Conference in Havana, Cuba. In December, 1936, the Eighth International Conference of American States was opened in Lima by the President of the United States, Franklin Delano Roosevelt.

This conference, held in Peru, and attended by President Roosevelt, was important for several reasons. In order to understand why these reasons are important we must go back to the earlier years of the Pan-American Union's existence.

Differences of race, language and custom, and in some cases religious differences, had helped to build up a feeling of aloofness between the peoples of the Central and South American countries and the United States. For many years there had been strained relations between Mexico and the United States. Little or nothing was done until 1889 to improve the relationships. The United States Government

had maintained a strangely indifferent attitude toward Pan-American conferences. This attitude of years' standing would be difficult to break down. Writers and journalists, especially in South America, were bitter in their criticisms of the coolness of America's strongest and largest nation. Then the Resolution adopted in 1930 to celebrate a Pan-

American Day, together with President Hoover's significant visit to Porto Rico, the "stepping-stone between Latin-America and the United States," began to create an entirely different attitude in our sister countries.

President Roosevelt's "good neighbor policy," as set forth in his historic "Good Neighbor" speech in 1933, began to lift the last curtain of doubt from the minds of the people of Latin-America. When Secretary of State Hull attended the seventh Annual Pan-American Conference, and President Roosevelt opened the Lima, Peru, Conference in December, 1936, and when all United States Marines were recalled from Central and South American countries, then at last the other members of the Union were convinced of our friendliness. The last wall of doubt and suspicion had been removed, and a new basis for friendship between our country and those nations of our neighbors was effected. The tone of the press in the Spanish and Portuguese papers of the South American Republics changed. Now they wrote without bitterness, without condemnation; with sympathy and understanding, and with buoyant hope for the future. Reserve and aloofness on both sides of the Gulf of Mexico had vanished. United States flags were flown with those of other American nations. With this attitude uppermost in the hearts and minds of the peoples of the nations involved, Pan-American Day has today the foundation it needs to cement everlasting friendship, co-operation and loyalty, and above all, understanding.

The Governing Board of the Pan-American Union consists of the Secretary of State of the United States, the Ambassadors, Ministers, and Charges d'Affaires in Washington of the twenty Latin-American countries. The twenty-one republics comprising the membership are as follows:

The United States of America, Mexico, Costa Rica, Salvador, Guatemala, Honduras, Nicaragua, Panama, Cuba, Dominican Republic, Haiti, Argentina, Bolivia, Brazil, Chile, Colombia, Ecuador, Paraguay, Peru, Uruguay, and Venezuela.

The Bulletin of the Pan-American Union is the official publication. Published in Washington, D. C., it keeps a complete record of the progress, history, education, and politics of the Pan-American countries. This periodical is issued in English, Spanish and Portuguese editions.

A Pan-American Union Building was built in Washington in 1910 by Andrew Carnegie. It is a very beautiful edifice and is visited by hundreds of thousands annually. Its chief interest to visitors is its magnificent tropical garden in a Latin-American courtyard, where colorful flowers and fountains give one a glimpse of the natural tropical beauty of the southern Republics represented by this building. It is more than likely that hundreds of school children at sight of this bit of Latin-America have made resolutions to visit the countries themselves. If and when they do, a magical world of wonder awaits them! Mexico, land of the Aztecs, home of the world's finest pottery, country of color and romance; Central America, with its islands of magical splendor, fine old cities and beautiful shores; South America, filled to overflowing with extravagant tropical beauty, well-planned gardens and natural landscapes.

Yearly on April 14th at the Pan-American Building there is a special concert of Latin-American music, singing and dancing, and special addresses. The gathering is attended by officials of the United States Government, members of the diplomatic corps, and others. The concert is always broadcast throughout the nation and is sent by short-wave to all American countries.

Another annual observance of the holiday is at Miami, Florida, where an impressive pageant depicts life in one of the Pan-American countries. In 1934 when Cuba was the subject of the pageant, the Mayor of Miami invited the Governor of Cuba to take part. Cuba sent her army and navy bands and Government representatives to attend the celebration.

In 1932, the bi-centennial of the birth of George Washington, the Governing Board of the Pan-American Union on April 14th made a pilgrimage to the tomb of Washington at Mount Vernon. Here messages were read by representatives of twenty-one of the Presidents of the member nations. No child in any one of those American Republics but who had heard of the Father of the first American Republic! It was entirely fitting that the 200th anniversary of his birth should be commemorated by representatives of those countries which had struggled for independence. They honored him as a great example of Americanism.

Philadelphia has observed Pan-American Day with much enthusiasm ever since its inauguration in 1931. This city has long been directly associated with South American republics because of its commerce and trade with them. A Pan-American Bulletin report points out that Philadelphia was one of the first cities of the United States to carry on trade with the southern Republics. At that time (1934) the city was still linked with them by thirteen steamship lines. This Bulletin also speaks of the gathering each year in Philadelphia, on July 14th at old St. Mary's Church, to pay tribute to the first Latin-American Minister to the United States, Manuel Torres, a resident of Philadelphia from 1796 until his death in 1822.

It has been emphasized by all countries of the Union that the educational observance of Pan-American Day is far more important than the oratory attendant upon it. It was in 1931 that the Governor of Cuba made the statement:

" The celebration of this day has been extended to the schools in order that our future citizens may learn as children to love their sister nations' by knowing their heroes, learning their customs, appreciating their virtues, and respecting their laws. The school is the soul of a country; it molds men, creates the civilization under which they shall live; it indicates the degree of national development and influences every section of civic life."

In 1933 a " Fountain of the Americas " was dedicated in Guatemala on Pan-American Day. Mexico, especially in the past few years, has celebrated Pan-American Day with ardent attention. A tablet dedicated to friendship between American peoples was unveiled in 1935, with appropriate ceremonies, on the International Bridge over the Rio Grande, between Laredo, Texas, and Nuevo Laredo, Mexico. In 1936 the Charles A. Lindbergh School of Mexico City put on a pageant in which school girls represented the twenty-one Republics of the Pan-American Union. In Chile, Argentina, Brazil, Peru, and other countries of South America, the day has been observed with fervor by the school children, at which time there are pageants, parades, music and dancing. At Havana, Cuba, a Diplomatic Reception on Pan-American Day is one of the important social affairs of the season.

The day has come to have a permanent place in the lives

of people all over the Western World. Instead of being merely an ideal, Pan-Americanism is a reality. Its permanence and its far-reaching influence can be assured by the continued celebration of this young but very important holiday. All who celebrate it will be contributing something toward a better understanding of, and sympathy with, the other inhabitants of a wonderful hemisphere. It was William Jennings Bryan who said:

" God has made us neighbors; let justice make us friends."

May 1

MAY DAY

Through many centuries and in many lands May Day has been observed with customs characteristic of the times and the people. Most of the celebrations have revolved around the May Pole. Even today on the first day of May we see it, gaily decorated with bright streamers of ribbon and surrounded by groups of dancing children or young women, the center of a May Queen Festival in our city parks or on some college campus.

An old Hungarian legend tells about the first May Pole, or May Tree as it is called in Hungary. May first is a Saint Day, dedicated to the Apostles St. Philip and St. James. The story goes that on a certain May Day centuries ago, a good Christian woman was walking forth with her staff in her hand when she was accosted by her enemies and accused of wrong-doing. The woman, knowing her innocence but being unable to prove it to her accusers, in desperation thrust her wooden staff into the ground and called upon the good Saints Philip and James to send some sign to prove her innocence. It is said that immediately her prayer was uttered, her staff sprouted green leaves and twigs and became a living, growing tree. From then on the May Tree was the symbolic center of May Day observances.

Many believe that May Day had its origin with the Druids because of their worship of the tree, and they trace its beginning back to the rites of the ancient Druid priests performed by them in honor of the god Bel. On the other hand it seems more likely that the custom of observing a festival at this time originated in ancient Rome. For here we see much similarity to the later May Day celebrations. The Roman festival was held in honor of Flora, goddess of flowers and springtime. It was known as Floralia, a joyous festival lasting from April 28th to May 3rd. At the beautiful Temple of Flora the celebrations were most significant. By tradition, the first to place a wreath or garland at the temple was assured of good luck throughout the coming year. Ropes of flowers were twined about its marble columns, while, all around the temple and on the streets, blossoms were thrown in great profusion by children and young women who were dressed in loose robes of white and wore flowers in their hair. The Floralia marked the beginning of spring and the Roman people celebrated it for several days.

The May Day Festival, whether a relic of the pagan Druids, or a carry-over of the Roman Floralia, was to the English people of the Middle Ages the happiest of the whole calendar! Although the day has been celebrated for several hundreds of years, at no time did it assume so much importance among the rural communities of England as in the Middle Ages. May Day has always been closest to the country folk for it is, after all, a true festival of Nature. All through the long, cold winter months the peasants looked forward to Spring. And when May Day came round Spring had really arrived in fullest array, with flowers and green-growing things in wood and field. This, then, was the time of the year when country people could rejoice in the fresh new beauty of their own land and realize anew what it meant to them. Flowers were a symbol of happiness, and green-growing things were symbolic of new life and new hope for the future. It was a time of joy, of song and dance to young and old. In every small village and rural community the people were off to the woods, returning at daybreak on May Day morn, laden down with boughs and blossoms. Thus they " brought home the May." And bringing home the May Tree was a most important part of the celebration. Historians tell us that the May Pole in some parishes of London was so huge that it took several yoke of oxen to draw it to the village. From an account of May

Day in Chambers' " Book of Days " we read: " Not content
with a garlanding of their brows, of their doors and win-
dows, these merry people of the old days had in every town,
or considerable district of a town, and in every village, a
fixed pole as high as the mast of a vessel of a hundred tons,
on which each May morning they suspended wreaths of
flowers, and round which they danced in rings pretty
nearly the whole day."

In some villages the May Pole was erected in front of
the church where it was believed to keep evil influences
from entering. From another historian of bygone days we
have a further account of the May Pole. " They have twenty
or forty yoke of oxen, every ox having a sweet nosegay of
flowers placed on the tip of his horns; and these oxen draw
home this Maypole which is covered all over with flowers
and herbs, bound round about with strings from top to the
bottom, and sometimes painted with variable colours, with
two or three hundred men, women and children following
it with great devotion. And thus being reared up, with
handkerchiefs and flags hovering on the top, they strew the
ground round about, bind green boughs about it, set up
summer halls, bowers and arbours hard by it, and fall they
to dance about it."

The procession at early morn on May Day from the woods
back to the village was gay with song and dance, jest and

laughter. Jolliest of all were the Morris dancers, they of the ribbons and streamers and bells at knee and toe, who performed with unceasing merriment to the great joy of the spectators. The Morris Dance is said to have originated centuries ago in Spain, but has come down to us with all the character of the English folk-dance. To a student of English peasant life it is characteristic of the joyous holiday spirit of the people.

In Somerset and Cornwall there was the hobby-horse dancer. He was an oddly grotesque figure of a man wearing a huge mask over his head to represent a horse, and nondescript draperies of all colors hanging down to conceal his feet. Accompanied by a drummer and an accordion player he went through all sorts of weird and comical antics, sending his audience into raptures of delight. He must have been a fantastic looking creature, for there is a legend telling how, many, many years ago, the town of Padstow in Cornwall was threatened by invasion from the French and when the invaders caught sight of the hobby-horse they fled!

It was the custom for all good housekeepers to have their housecleaning done by the time May Day came round, and one thing necessary to a clean house was a clean chimney! In those days of huge fireplaces and gigantic chimneys, there were small urchins whose work was to climb up the chimneys with their brooms, at the bidding of their masters, and sweep out the black soot of a winter's accumulation. Tom, the chimney-sweep in *The Water-Babies* by Charles Kingsley, was one of these. On May Day all the chimney-sweeps took part in the Procession. They danced and sang and collected pennies, and a strange sight they must have been with their ragged, sooty clothes in the midst of the well-dressed villagers. But since they were to be rewarded after the parade with a dinner of roast beef and plum pudding, it is safe to wager that none missed being there! Another group in the parade was comprised of milkmaids. They paraded with their cows; both maids and cows were festooned with ribbons and blossoms. Stage-coaches and horses were also there, trimmed all over in every place where a flower or streamer could be fastened. One extraordinary feature of every May Day parade was the " Jack-in-the-green," usually to be found with the chimney-sweeps. " Jack-in-the-green " was, literally, Jack enclosed within a green bower—a light framework of wood in which he was almost completely hidden by green boughs and flowers. The frame and its occupant were carried on the shoulders of several men. Just how this feature of May Day parades originated is not known.

There were many superstitions connected with May Day. One of the most popular was that of hanging whitethorn over one's door to keep out the witches! Another practice among the girls and young women of the village was that of bathing their faces in the morning dew on May Day morn, which was believed to assure them of lovely complexions for the coming year. In Ireland dew was sometimes collected and placed in bottles and applied when needed, for it was thought to have healing powers. It was said that a heavy dew on the first of May was the sign of a good butter year. The Irish went to great pains to help along a good yield of butter; clay was removed from the split of a cow's hoof and placed with a coal of fire and a bit of salt under the butter churn! Then the witches were defied. Witches were almost as conspicuous on the eve of May Day as on Hallowe'en. " If you dare to tease the cat on this night, don't be surprised if it turns into a witch! " One sure way for mortal man to be able to see the old women on May Eve was to put his clothes on wrong side out and walk backward to the nearest crossroad—if he had the courage!

Even the ancient Romans had a superstition against marrying in May. Said Ovid: " If you regard old saws, mind, thus they say: 'Tis bad to marry in the month of May." An old English maxim on this subject tells us:

Marry in May,
You'll rue the day,
To marry in May,
Is to wed povertie.

At the time of the Puritans, May Day lost much of its popularity in England and was observed only surreptitiously because of the ban on all such frivolities. Many or most of the May Poles were uprooted when Parliament in 1644 made them unlawful. But, after the Restoration, May Day came into its own again. Never again, however, was the holiday so wholeheartedly celebrated as it had been before the Puritans.

Choosing a May Queen for the May Day festivities has existed since May Day celebrations had their beginning, and is one custom of this holiday that has not been lost. During the first days of May there are fairs and festivals held in towns throughout all of England; over each of these a May Queen presides. On the first Sunday following May Day there is the great London May Queen Festival held at Hayes Common, near Kent. Here are assembled all the beautiful May Queens of the lesser festivals. From these lovely girls one is chosen " May Queen of London " and she is crowned with elaborate ceremony and presides over the festival.

In some of the outlying districts of London, small children still go about on May Day carrying a doll dressed in white,—the Lady of the May. Going from house to house they sing carols and give away the flowers they carry, expecting pennies in return. When there is a knock at the door and the lady of the house sees the children wreathed in smiles and holding forth small nosegays of flowers, she realizes that it is May Day and that a half penny is expected of her.

Although May Day seems to belong more appropriately to England than anywhere else, it is observed in other countries in various ways.

In some parts of Europe, May Day Eve is known as Walpurgis Night, and fires are kindled with great hilarity " to burn out the witches." * In the Highlands of Scotland Beltane Fires are lit on the hilltops, a relic of the Druid rites in honor of the god Bel. In Scotland and Ireland today there are still the old wishing wells. A wish made at the wishing well on May Day will surely come true! And in Ireland it is said that if a girl sees her lover's reflection as she makes her wish, and if it be just at sunrise on May Day, she will be married to him before the year is out, and it is said, too, that a maid of Dublin, if she wishes to see her future husband on the morrow, places a stocking filled with yarrow under her pillow the night before May Day. There was a special verse to be chanted over this ritual:

Good morrow, good yarrow, good morrow to thee;
I hope 'gain the morrow my lover to see,

---

* Walpurgis was an early missionary to Germany, born in England in the eighth century. Walpurgis Night is observed in various countries at various times, but usually on May Eve.

And that he may be married to me;
The colour of his hair, and the clothes he does wear;
And if he be for me may his face be turned to me;
And if he be not, dark and surly may he be,
And his back turned to me.

—From Notes and Queries.

Because of the scarcity of timber in Ireland, the May Pole has not been used there for years, although in some places the small mountain ash is brought into the village for this purpose. But everywhere on May Day there are flowers, lilacs and hawthorn, and great fields of golden gorse in fullest bloom. Primroses gathered before sunrise and strewn about the house bring good luck to that house, or better still, a bunch tied to the cow's tail! The Irish peasant folk have many pleasant superstitions relating to May Day. On May Eve the " wee people " are very active. They play their fairy pipes and can easily be heard by those who have the courage to seek them out, although it is said that they who listen to such sweet music are not long for this earth. Many are the strange sights that have been seen on the first day of May. Enchanted cities in a midst of magic rise up from the sea in all the sparkling beauty of the past ages. It is said, too, that O'Donoghue of Killarney comes up from his castle under the waters and rides upon a snow-white steed, a retinue of lords and ladies following him.

In modern Greece the May Day fêtes are celebrated with girls in traditional white robes doing the graceful, classic dances that have made Greek dances famous for centuries. All the schools are given a holiday and practically everyone spends it in the woods, where wild flowers are gathered and fashioned into wreaths. These wreaths are taken home and hung up until the Eve of St. John, June 23rd, when they are burned in the great bonfires that are kindled according to tradition for that purpose.

May Day in Italy is for the most part a day of sports meets, races and contests of all kinds. In Modena, however, the day is known as the Maytime of the Maidens, and is a very romantic day indeed. This is the time for young lovers to serenade their sweethearts. When a girl is serenaded by her swain standing beneath her window, it is a pretty sure sign that the two will wed before the year is out. In Switzerland the *Maitannli* or May Pine Tree is placed under the sweetheart's window. They say that if the girl is quite unpopular she may find instead of the gaily decorated *Maitannli* an ugly straw man—a veritable scarecrow!

Huge fires are kindled in Sweden on May Eve to keep the witches away. These fires in Stockholm, on Reindeer Mountain, are made from great piles of logs, barrels and boxes, and the light from their blaze can be seen for miles around. One of the old customs of Sweden was that of sprinkling grass on the doorsteps to keep out the witches who roamed on that night. The witches had to count the blades of grass before entering, giving those inside fair warning.

In a great many places flowers are exchanged on May Day. In Denmark lovers exchange wreaths made from a dried plant. In Poland boys and girls carry twigs of green from house to house which they sell for a few cents. These sprigs of green are supposed to bring good luck to the house, especially to cattle and crops. The French have a custom of exchanging *muguets*—nosegays of lilies-of-the-valley. Making a wish while wearing a *muguet* from a friend, is supposed to make the wish come true.

In France on May Day one sees small children collecting pennies " for the May." One will have been chosen to represent the Virgin of the May. They dress her in a robe of white and crown her with a wreath of flowers. Then, surrounded on her throne by other little girls, she is the center of a picture which is thought to be worthy of a donation of small coins from passers-by. One very old custom in the vicinity of Paris is that of drinking May milk at dawn on May Day—milk that is still warm and foaming, fresh from the cow.

In the United States May Day has never had the same background of tradition and custom that it has enjoyed in

England and other countries where it is celebrated. Whatever customs were brought to America from England in colonial times were straightway destroyed by the Puritans in New England. Nathaniel Hawthorne tells of an attempted celebration round a May Pole in Massachusetts in the early days of that colony. The Governor was so enraged by the demonstration that he hacked the pole to pieces with his sword.

The May Day customs here, therefore, are those retained from early English settlers who dared to carry out the old practices, and those people from other countries who have settled in America during the past few generations. In Chicago, for instance, the Greek dances of May Day are performed by the Greek population and are fast becoming traditional. In Palo Alto, California, there has been for years a May Day Festival for children. The novelist, Kathleen Norris, has been its chairman and inspiration for a long time, making it one of the most joyous occasions of the year for little folks.

One rather universal observance of May Day in the United States are those fêtes held everywhere on college campuses throughout the country. Dancing about a May Pole with a May Queen presiding and her ladies-in-waiting in attendance is one tradition that we hope will never die out. The one held at Bryn Mawr College in Pennsylvania is perhaps the most famous of all. At Wellesley College the seniors hold a hoop-rolling contest in connection with their outdoor festival on May Day.

Quite often on the green mall of city parks and at some of the city playgrounds we see the May Pole on the first of May with its ribbon streamers and children dancing round it. Green grass and the scent of flowers, and sun shining down upon the youthful dancers and upon the May Queen who is crowned with flowers and wreathed in smiles at the honor bestowed upon her! The scene is not so different from those May festivities of four or five hundred years ago. It is a custom too full of meaning and too steeped in tradition—tradition of the ancient Roman Floralia, and countless generations of English people who honored May Day, and people everywhere who recognized the hope and joy of another spring—to be permitted to go out of existence. Let us hope that it never will!

May

MOTHER'S DAY

A certain Hebrew proverb says: "God could not be everywhere; therefore He made mothers." Observing a day in
honor of our mothers is comparatively a new idea in this
country. But many years ago the people of England had such
a day. It was called Mothering Sunday. Observed on a
Mid-Lent Sunday, the day was kept by visiting one's mother
and taking her a gift—usually a delicacy called *simnel*
cake. An old poem from Herrick's *Hesperides* mentions it.

> *I'll to thee a Simnel bring*
> *'Gainst thou go'st a-mothering;*

So that when she blesseth thee,
Half that blessing thou'lt give me.

The Yugoslavs have a quaint Mother's Day,—*Materitse*—
when the children of a family bind up their mother and
won't let her go until she has promised them something
good to eat! The same custom is observed on Mother Feast
Day in Serbia where the mother has hidden little gifts under
her pillow for the children.

The first suggestion for a special commemorative day in
this country, as far as we know, came from the writer of
that famous classic of the Civil War, " Battle Hymn of the
Republic." Julia Ward Howe's idea was to establish Independence Day as a Mother's Day, making it a day of peace.
The suggestion apparently was never taken seriously. Later
in 1904 at a convention of the Eagles Lodge at South Bend,
Indiana, a proposal was made by one of the members, Frank
E. Hering, that a day be set aside each year to honor
mothers.

But the real founder was Miss Anna Jarvis of Philadelphia. Wishing to honor the memory of her own mother,
Miss Jarvis conceived the idea of observing a day in each
year to honor mothers everywhere. To that end she worked
for many years, traveling thousands of miles, making
speeches, writing letters, and giving all her time and effort

to the cause. Finally after having spent two years in Washington, Miss Jarvis saw her dream realized when, on May 8, 1914, President Wilson signed a joint resolution in Congress in which he ordered that the second Sunday in May be observed each year as Mother's Day, authorizing the display of the flag on all government buildings on that date. On that first official Mother's Day President Wilson wore a white carnation in his lapel as a mark of respect for mothers.

The custom of wearing carnations on Mother's Day is part of the story of Miss Jarvis's mother. Mrs. Anna Reeves Jarvis was the mother of eleven children, wife of a minister, and proud owner of a garden on the grounds of their home in West Virginia. Known all over town for her great kind heart, Mrs. Jarvis found real pleasure in distributing flowers to those who had none. It was because of this passion for flowers that her daughter, years later, chose one as a symbol of " the Mother of Mother's Day," and selected a carnation.

In writing about Miss Anna Jarvis in " Mother of Mother's Day," Ann Hark has this to say concerning the choice of a white carnation: " The whiteness of the blossom . . . represents the purity of motherhood, the calyx symbolizes life, its fragrance is like the incense of a mother's prayers, its wide field of growth exemplifies the boundless charity of a mother's love; its enduring characteristics, her fidelity. And, crowning touch of all, the carnation's habit of folding its faded petals to its heart instead of dropping them, . . . illustrates as no other picture could the undying quality of a mother's love."

In establishing the custom of Mother's Day Miss Jarvis stressed the importance of sending a message to Mother on her Day. The occasion has become commercialized to such an extent that telegrams conveying appropriate sentiments are now available at special rates; and shops, department stores, drug stores, flower shops and other places where gifts can be bought are lavish in their displays, reminding the buyer to purchase a gift for Mother on Mother's Day. However, the day itself is heartily welcomed by individuals everywhere who want to take this special opportunity of showing some gratitude to Mother.

After realizing her dream in America, Miss Jarvis turned her attention to other countries hoping to make the day one of international observance. Her idea took root almost instantly abroad—in England, France, Sweden, Denmark, Hawaii and the Sandwich Islands, Samoa, China, Japan, India, Palestine and other countries from one end of the globe to the other. In Mexico the holiday lasts two days.

Tree-planting has been a popular feature of Mother's Day programs. On that day in Washington trees have been planted in honor of American mothers and the mothers of the Presidents of the United States. In Los Angeles there is a park called Mother's Memory Garden in which the California Mother's Tree is planted.

In honor of the day a special United States postage stamp was issued in 1934 bearing the world-famous picture of Whistler's Mother.

A great deal has been done to keep the observance of Mother's Day alive by the Golden Rule Mother's Day Committee of the Golden Rule Foundation. Every year this committee, aside from sponsoring essay contests on the subject, selects one woman in America as the typical American mother. This "mother" takes part in the Mother's Day program which is broadcast throughout the nation.

In observing the second Sunday in May we are doing more than just showing our love for our mother. We are giving expression to a feeling of respect and reverence for all mothers everywhere—those now living and those who have passed on. Many of them have blessed the world with sons and daughters who have made great contributions to civilization. "All that I am or hope to be, I owe to my angel mother. Blessings on her memory," said Lincoln. Years later another famous American spoke thus: "My mother was the making of me," said Edison. "She was so true, so sure of me, and I felt I had someone to live for, someone I must not disappoint."

Most beloved of all famous mothers is Mary, Mother of

Jesus. Gentle, loving and pure, she symbolizes the sacredness of mother-love through the ages, and we see her today wherever the spiritual light of love shines through a mother's eyes.

June

CHILDREN'S DAY

There are several days of the calendar that might be called Children's Day. First of all there is a Children's Day observed in most Protestant churches. Started by the Methodist Episcopal Church in June, 1868, when the custom began to be observed annually, it was gradually adopted by other churches. On the second Sunday in June the church service is given over to the Sunday School; the children march into the church from their Sunday-School rooms and every class is represented by special Children's Day exercises.

Another and much older children's church festival is Childermas, observed in Greek, Roman and Anglican churches. Childermas, also known as the Feast of the Innocents, is taken from the account of the massacre of children in the time of Herod. From the Book of Matthew: " Then Herod, when he saw that he was mocked of the wise men, was exceeding wroth, and sent forth and slew all the children that were in Bethlehem. And in all the coasts thereof, from two years old and under, according to the time which he had diligently inquired of the wise men." Childermas—December 28th—is considered an unlucky day on the calendar. There was a time in England when it was certainly unlucky for boys and girls, for that day was chosen to flog the children to make them good! The Puritans of the early New England colonies apparently held the same belief, for a writer of that period tells us: " It hath been a custom to whip up the children on Holy Innocents' Day morning, that the memories of this murther might stick the closer." On the other hand, a custom of Belgium made the Festival of the Innocents a happy day for youngsters, for the parents allowed them on that day to do almost anything they pleased and, furthermore, to give orders to their elders instead of receiving them!

The Feast of St. Sava is a glad day for the children of Serbia—a holiday that is looked forward to all the year. St. Sava was a king's son who died January 14, 1236, and since that time January 14th has been kept as a Children's Day in Serbia in commemoration of the good work St. Sava did for children. After celebrations in the schools in honor of the man who built schools, churches and monasteries all over Serbia, the day ends with feasting, music, and dancing.

Dechivi Dan is the Children's Day of Yugoslavia when the children are tied up by their parents and not set free until they promise to be good all the rest of the year!

December 21st, or St. Thomas's Day, is observed in Belgium by a peculiar custom. The boys and girls are put out of the house and the doors are locked. Then the older members of the family call to them through the window: " St. Thomas's Day! St. Thomas's Day! What will you give to come in? " And the children must pay a forfeit to get back into the house.

The Festival of Dolls in Japan is a very old holiday, and an important one in that country, for the Japanese consider that the doll plays a very important rôle in the happiness of their children. The festival, according to our calendar, comes about the end of April. All the little girls fondly display their dolls, many of them receive new ones on this day, and all the dolls in Japan are fêted! Early in June there is a day called the Burial of the Broken Dolls when, with great ceremony, all the dolls that are too badly broken to be mended are buried with Buddhist rites with real priests officiating. After the little girls have placed their dolls, some without arms and legs, some with heads missing, into the one big grave, they sing the " Song of the Broken Dolls " and seem far from sad. Perhaps they know that by the time the Doll Festival comes round they will have new dolls.

A brand new holiday in Japan is " Children's Protection Day," started in 1922 after the modern calendar had been accepted by the nation. Observed annually on April 17th it is a day commemorating the passing of a legal enactment for caring for juvenile delinquents. This law provides that, instead of being sent to court and to houses of detention, the boys and girls who have proven to be delinquent are placed under the supervision of chosen schools for proper guidance.

The United States now celebrates a very important Children's Day, and that is May the first, proclaimed annually by the President as Child Health Day. Although New York had a Child Health Bureau as early as 1908, and other cities soon afterward, the work was dropped during the World War. However, after the war the American Child Health Association urged its reorganization. Sponsored also by the Children's Bureau of the United States Department of Labor, and by the Departments of Education in the various states, Child Health Day is annually a successful reality. The first observance of the day was in 1924. In 1928 a Congressional Resolution was adopted stating: " That May 1st shall hereafter be designated and known as May Day Child Health Day and that it shall be the duty of the President to request its observance as provided in this resolution." The day is especially celebrated in the schools with exercises and prize contests for essays on the subject of Health. One very satisfying result of these years of making the public conscious of child health is the fact that Health is now taught in the schools all the year round, and is not reserved simply for one special day of the year.

May 30

MEMORIAL DAY

Your silent tents of green
We deck with fragrant flowers;
Yours has the suffering been,
The memory shall be ours.
                    —Henry W. Longfellow.

Most countries have one day in the year set apart for honoring the dead. That day in the United States is to keep alive the memories of those who have fallen for their country. But because it started immediately after the Civil War it has been devoted mostly to veterans of that war. Now, however, the aged soldiers of that period in history are fast disappearing from among us. In addition to the graves of those who fought in the Civil War there are those of soldiers of the Spanish-American and the World War to be remembered at this time. "These men have died that we might live." It is natural for the heart of man to grieve over those departed, and fitting and proper that their memories be kept alive.

The first observance of this day, often called by the Northern States Decoration Day, was on May 30, 1868. It began when several women in the South decorated with flowers the graves of both Confederate and Union soldiers. The reason for their choosing May 30th has been explained in this way: in France the thirtieth of May has been observed as a legal holiday for many years to commemorate the day when Napoleon's ashes were brought to France from St. Helena. Called " The Day of the Ashes " it is a memorial day to France's greatest general. It is said that the first Memorial Day in America was observed more or less through the efforts of a woman from Virginia whose name was Cassandra Oliver Moncure. If she was French as her name suggests, it is easy to understand why she might choose the French " Day of the Ashes " to observe our own day of memorial.

In order to establish a fixed time for Memorial Day, it was suggested to the National Commander of the Grand Army of the Republic that he set a specific day for decorating the graves of the Union soldiers. Therefore General Logan, the Commander, named May 30th to be set aside " for the purpose of strewing with flowers or otherwise decorating the graves of comrades who died in defense of their country during the late rebellion, and with the hope that it will be kept up from year to year."

This custom *was* kept up by those comrades and others, and especially by the Sons of Veterans of America. May 30th is now a legal holiday in all of the Northern States and in the Possessions of the United States. In North and South Carolina Memorial Day is observed May 10th, while in Alabama, Florida, Georgia, and Mississippi it is observed on April 26th. Still other Southern States celebrate June 3rd, June 6th, and June 9th.

In every town and city of the United States people go to the cemeteries on Memorial Day to visit and decorate the graves of the nation's soldiers with flowers and American flags. In many places there are parades, assemblies, dinners and speeches to celebrate the day. Probably the most repeated speech at this time is Lincoln's Gettysburg Address, and one of the most important of the country's memorial parks is the Battleground of Gettysburg.

At the 75th anniversary of the Battle of Gettysburg held July 1, 2, 3, 1938, a celebration on the battleground was attended by 1,800 surviving veterans of the Civil War, of the G. A. R. and the Confederate Army. Guests of the Government, they came from all over the United States, north and south, east and west. On July 2nd before a gathering of 150,000 persons, President Franklin D.

Roosevelt dedicated a monument on Oak Hill, called the
Eternal Light Peace Memorial. A Union soldier of the
G. A. R. and a Confederate soldier from Georgia unveiled
the shaft rising fifty feet above the ground, topped by a
steadily burning flame visible for a distance of twenty
miles. The inscription on the monument reads: " An enduring light to guide us in unity and fellowship."

Each year on Memorial Day the National Cemetery at
Arlington, Virginia, is the scene of an impressive ceremony,
as are also the other National cemeteries throughout the
nation.

There is a beautiful custom observed in all the important
ports of the United States, in which those who have died in
battle at sea are honored in a picturesque ceremony. Tiny
ships laden with flowers are set afloat upon the water to
honor these brave heroes of the nation's navy. This custom
is similar to one in China and Japan which takes place during the Feast of the Dead, when candles are lighted and
sent out upon the waves on small flat bits of wood as a
light for the souls of those who have died at sea.

In recent years Memorial Day has also been Poppy Day,
in most of the forty-eight states as well as in other countries
where there are veterans of the World War. These tiny red
artificial poppies, marked *Honor the Dead by helping the
Living,* are sold by ex-service men for the benefit of disabled

veterans. The idea originated in France, although the poppy has now become a familiar symbol in England, Canada, the United States, Australia, and New Zealand.

While the American soldiers were still in France after the World War there were several notable Memorial Day services held " over there." Of these, that held at Suresnes Cemetery near Paris on May 30, 1919, was probably the most impressive. President Wilson made the address, an appeal to all countries to join the League of Nations. The dream of his heart, that of seeing the United States become a member, never materialized. " It is for us," he said in that address, " particularly for us who are civilized, to use our proper weapons of counsel and agreement to see to it that there never is such a war again."

During the years after the War the graves of American soldiers were decorated by the French as well as by the Americans. In May of 1922, in observance of the American Memorial Day, two million boys and girls in the French schools wrote essays on America's help to the French in the Great War. In one of these a little girl from the Somme wrote: " When I go walking with Mamma on Sunday, I put a pretty little bouquet of flowers on the grave of an American, and if there are any weeds I pull them out."

Decorating graves is an ancient custom, having been observed by the Druids and the ancient Greeks and Romans.

At the Parentalia, the Romans placed garlands of flowers on the graves of the dead. Today the Italians observe All Souls, at which time prayers are said for the souls of the departed.

France annually observes *Jour des Morts* when everybody carries wreaths to the graves, and the cemeteries are bright with flowers. Even the graves of the unknown are not forgotten. The Roumanians celebrate a Memorial Day the day after ours, on the Eve of the Trinity, when presents are given away in exchange for prayers for the living as well as for the dead. There is a Memorial Day in Yugoslavia to commemorate the execution of the country's two leading patriots, Count Peter Zrinski and Marquis Francis Frankopan. In the East Indies and parts of China graves are decorated on a day known as *Ching Ming,* or the Festival of the Tombs.

FLAG DAY

June 14

I pledge allegiance to my Flag and to the Republic for which it stands.
One nation indivisible, with liberty and justice for all.

For nearly fifty years this pledge to the American Flag has been repeated by millions of school children and other citizens in their salute to the Flag. Written by James B. Upham, of the *Youth's Companion* magazine staff, it first came into prominence at the World's Columbian Exposition in Chicago, in 1892. And now, standing at attention, right hand raised in salute, we repeat that solemn pledge, giving allegiance to the flag that protects us. The flag.

Why should we pledge allegiance to a flag, a bit of decorated bunting on a stick? What does it mean? Everyone knows, of course, that the flag is a symbol of our country. It has come to mean so much to us through the years since its adoption by the Nation in 1777,—so much more than just a banner— that the Stars and Stripes as it waves in the breeze seems to us the soul and spirit of the land we love.

Appropriate to our love and respect for our flag we observe Flag Day, honoring the Stars and Stripes.

The history of our flag begins with the history of our country as a nation. In 1775 the Continental Congress appointed a committee for the purpose of choosing a flag, this committee comprising Benjamin Franklin, Thomas Lynch and Benjamin Harrison. The result was that on June 14, 1777, the following resolution was adopted by Congress: " *Resolved,* That the flag of the United States be thirteen stripes, alternate red and white, that the ' Union ' be thirteen stars, white in a blue field, representing a new constellation."

There have been several reasons advanced as to why red, white and blue were chosen for the American flag. In studying the types of flags that were in use at that time we can see that there were probably a number of factors which influenced our own. Some historians have pointed out that the colors were chosen because the white signified purity and innocence; the red, hardiness and valor; the blue, perseverance, vigilance, and justice. Granting that, there were reasons why stripes were chosen, and stars in a blue field. It is certain that prior to 1777 there was no one flag that could be called the Union flag. It is said, for instance, that in New York in 1775 " A Union flag with a red field was hoisted at New York upon the liberty-pole, bearing the inscription, ' George Rex, and the Liberties of America.' " Another flag was described by a London magazine of 1776: " The colors of the American fleet were striped upon the Union, with thirteen strokes, called the United Colonies, and their standard, a rattlesnake; motto—' Don't tread on me.' " Another flag that was popular with the Colonies was the Pine Tree Flag. On it were the words: *" An appeal to Heaven."*

In 1775 the Philadelphia Light Horse Company was using a flag with alternate blue and silver stripes in the upper left-hand corner. The following year another flag appeared which represented the union of the colonies. From the British Annual Register of 1776 this flag is referred to as follows: " They (the Colonies) are said to have changed their colors from a plain red ground, which they had hitherto used, to a flag with thirteen stripes, as a symbol of the number and union of the colonies." Elsewhere this flag is described as having a blue field containing the Cross of

St. George and St. Andrew. One thing is certain, that red and white were chosen because they had been used by the colonies in the flag of England; the blue was probably used because it was a background for the stars "representing a new constellation" and because blue was a popular color in the American Colonies.

We have on record these words from George Washington concerning the new flag: "We take the star from Heaven, the red from our mother country, separating it by white stripes, thus showing that we have separated from her, and the white stripes shall go down to posterity representing liberty."

It is believed that a five-pointed star was chosen to grace the blue field of our flag because it was used by our Allies, France and Holland, while the six-pointed star was used by England.

Thirteen stripes were chosen, as were the thirteen stars, to represent the thirteen colonies that had become states. When new states were added to the Union, a new problem presented itself, and so a change was made. In 1795 two new stars were added to the blue field, and two new stripes, these representing Vermont and Kentucky. Until 1812 this 15-stars and 15-stripes arrangement was the national flag. Then five new states were added—Tennessee, Ohio, Louisiana, Indiana and Mississippi. Should a new stripe and a new star be added to the flag for each of these states?

In 1818 Congress enacted a new law concerning the national flag.

> "*Section 1.* . . . That from and after the fourth day of July next, the flag of the United States be thirteen horizontal stripes, alternate red and white; that the Union have twenty stars, white in a blue field."

> "*Section 2.* . . . That on the admission of every new state into the Union one star be added to the Union of the flag, and that such addition shall take effect on the Fourth of July next succeeding such admission."

In studying the history of the American flag, it is not until the year 1870 that we find any mention of Betsy Ross as the maker of the first American flag. In that year Betsy Ross's grandson told the story, that is now familiar to nearly everyone, of how George Washington, accompanied by Robert Morris and George Ross, called upon Mrs. Betsy Ross, a widow residing at 239 Arch Street in Philadelphia, and asked her to make the newly adopted flag. It is said that she was shown the design and agreed to make the flag, and that with her scissors she cut them a five-pointed star showing Mr. Washington how it would look on the flag. Although there is no documentary evidence to support the

Betsy Ross story, it is a legend that has been accepted by the American people, and Betsy Ross's name is synonymous with the making of the American flag. Her home on Arch Street is a shrine in Philadelphia that has been visited by hundreds of thousands since the Betsy Ross Memorial Association was founded in 1898. The house was purchased in 1905.

The United States is probably the only nation whose National Anthem is written around the flag, although it was 117 years after the song had been written that it was officially accepted as the American National Anthem. Although "The Star-Spangled Banner" was almost universally considered to be the National Anthem, Congress was hesitant about making it official, probably because "My Country 'Tis of Thee" was more popular in some sections of the country, particularly in the New England States. Chiefly through the efforts of the National Star-Spangled Banner Commission, organized in 1914 on the one hundredth anniversary of the writing of the song, it was finally accepted, an act of Congress in March 1931 making it the National Anthem.

It was the flag flown from Fort McHenry, during the War of 1812, that inspired Francis Scott Key to write his immortal song. That flag, measuring thirty by forty feet, is now in the National Museum at Washington. Frayed with age, and with one star cut from the blue field, it remains a mute reminder of that night of battle.

On the night of September 13, 1814, Francis Scott Key had obtained permission to go to the British fleet in the harbor to plead for the pardon of a friend of his family, who was being held prisoner on some minor charge. He reached the British ship safely and was successful in obtaining the pardon. Getting away from the ship was a different matter, however, for suddenly the bombardment of Fort McHenry began, and Key was forced to stay on the British ship. When dawn broke and he could see the American flag waving, he knew that the Fort was still in the hands of his countrymen. It was then he wrote the song, on the back of an old envelope, calling it " The Defense of Fort McHenry." Later it was printed and distributed to stir up patriotism, and soon afterward, the war having been won, it became a popular song of victory.

The first Flag Day in America was observed on June 14, 1877. That year Congress requested that the flag be flown from all public buildings to commemorate the one hundredth birthday of the American flag. In 1894 a Flag Day Association was formed in Chicago. This Association named the third Saturday in June as Flag Day, but two years later the date was changed back to June 14th, it being the actual anniversary of the day the American Flag was adopted.

From that time on cities and public officials observed the day, and soon it began to be celebrated in the schools. Today school children are taught not only the history of their flag but also the formalities concerning it, or " flag etiquette." It is unlawful to desecrate the American flag in any way, and no true citizen would wilfully do such a thing. There are definite formalities to be observed in showing proper respect to the flag. At a National Flag Conference held in Washington on Flag Day in 1923, a flag code was drawn up, a code which is too long to include in this chapter.

The saying that " the sun never sets on the American flag " is true. From Alaska to the Panama Canal, from the Philippines to the Virgin Islands, and from the northernmost tip of Maine to the Samoan Islands, the Stars and Stripes waves proudly, a symbol of the land of the free.

" Our flag carries American ideas, American history, and American feelings. Beginning with the Colonies and coming down to our time, in its sacred heraldry, in its glorious insignia, it has gathered and stored chiefly this supreme idea—divine right of liberty in man. Every color means liberty, every thread means liberty, every form of star and beam or stripe of light means liberty; not lawlessness, not license, but organized, institutional liberty—liberty through law, and law for liberty." Thus a great American preacher,

Henry Ward Beecher, wrote of the Stars and Stripes of America.

FLAG " FIRSTS "

First salute accorded the Stars and Stripes by another nation was by France when Captain John Paul Jones shipped at a French port on the *Ranger*, February 14, 1778.

☆

Stars and Stripes first admitted on equality with flags of other nations on September 3, 1783.

☆

First American flag to fly over a schoolhouse was in 1812, at the small log schoolhouse in Catamount Hills, Massachusetts.

☆

First Flag Day observance was June 14, 1877.

First Flag Day observed by schools was in the Philadelphia Public Schools in 1893.

First Flag Day Association was formed in Chicago in 1894.

First National Conference on the display and respect of the flag met on Flag Day in Washington in 1919.

☆

First Flag Week was held May 23rd to 30th, 1926, " to inculcate and promote greater love and respect " for the American flag.

July 4

INDEPENDENCE DAY

The Fourth of July, a legal holiday in all the forty-eight states and all territories and possessions of the United States of America, commemorates the birth of a great nation.

On June 28, 1776, the Declaration of Independence, having been drawn up by Thomas Jefferson, was presented to Congress and was adopted on July 4th. But it was not until August 2nd that all the fifty-six signers had placed their names on the copy of the Declaration which had been engrossed on parchment. With *courage,* and faith *in their right to freedom,* the colonies severed their relations with Britain by engaging in a war which gave them their independence. The colonies became the United States of America, a republic which was to grow rapidly and magnificently into one of the greatest nations of the world.

"We, therefore, the Representatives of the United States of America," the final paragraph of the Declaration of Independence reads: "in General Congress, Assembled, appealing to the Supreme Judge of the world for the rectitude of our intentions do, in the Name, and by authority of the good People of these Colonies, solemnly publish and declare, That these United Colonies are, and of Right ought to be, Free and Independent States: that they are Absolved from all Allegiance to the British Crown, and that all political connections between them and the State of Great Britain is and ought to be totally dissolved: and that as Free and Independent States, they have full Power to levy War, conclude Peace, contract Alliances, establish Commerce, and to do all other Acts and Things which Independent States may of right do. And for the support of this Declaration, with a firm reliance on the protection of Divine Providence, we mutually pledge to each other our Lives, our Fortunes, and our sacred Honor."

The birthday of any nation should be the proudest holiday of that nation! No country in history has had more reason to be proud of its beginning than our own. Born of the desire for freedom, nurtured by faith and courage, founded on the highest principles and ideals conceivable to man, it has faced and fought wars and civil strife, economic depressions and political vicissitudes, to emerge rich and resourceful, mighty in the world and infallible as a nation. Nowhere in the world have individuals the freedom and opportunity that belong to an American citizen. Richard Henry Lee had declared, in a resolution presented to Congress: " that these United Colonies are, and of right ought to be, free and independent states." That aspiration fought and won freedom for the people in the Colonies and that precious heritage was given to us and to all future Americans.

The first celebration of Independence Day centered, naturally enough, in the city of Philadelphia where the Declaration was signed the year before. Philadelphia was then the capital of the nation. Regardless of the fact that war was going on, there was a hearty celebration on that first birthday of national independence. Congress gave a dinner to military officers and the city fathers, bands played and all the city was gay with bunting, even to the ships in the harbor. Already the prophecy of John Adams was coming true. In a letter to his wife the year before, when the Declaration was accepted by Congress, he had expressed his belief in the importance of the day. " I am apt to believe that it will be celebrated by succeeding generations as the great anniversary festival," he wrote. " It ought to be commemorated as the day of deliverance, by solemn acts of devotion to God Almighty. It ought to be solemnized with pomp and parade, with shows, games, sports, guns, bells, bonfires, and illuminations, from one end of this continent to the other, from this time forward evermore." Philadelphia, at least, and probably many other towns of the new nation, observed the day through the years of the Revolution and from then on to the present time. In the year 1826 Independence Day was celebrated as usual, but sadness was mingled with the rejoicing, for that day saw the death of two of the most famous signers of the Declaration of Independence, Thomas Jefferson and John Adams.

The peak of Independence Day celebrations in Philadelphia was in 1926, when that city held a Sesqui-Centennial in honor of the 150th year of independence. Every state and territory of the United States and many nations of the world participated in the event, and people from all corners of America came to visit the birthplace of the nation, the home of Independence Hall and the Liberty Bell.

One phase of Fourth of July celebrations is passing out of existence—the practice of setting off explosive fireworks. Independence Day has always been celebrated with plenty of noise,—bands and parades, gun- and cannon-firing, and fireworks of all kinds. Every year the day was marked by hundreds of people being killed and thousands injured. At the beginning of the twentieth century the peril was at its height. As early as 1907 the fatalities for July 4th from fireworks amounted to more than 1100 persons, with twice that many injured. After protests were made and people were warned each year of the danger, the casualties dropped somewhat, but still on July 5th each year the newspapers all over the country carried stories of dead and injured. There are laws restricting the sale of fireworks in more than twenty states and in over 500 cities, and several states forbid the sale of fireworks entirely. Eventually, it is hoped, all states will adopt similar measures to safeguard life and property. With the passing of firecrackers Independence Day has taken on a new character. The holiday has assumed a more peaceful mien, and more attention is given the patriotic aspects of the nation's birthday.

In 1918 Independence Day was observed in England for the first time. This observance, by the British, of a day commemorating the severance of the American colonies from the mother country marked an epoch in the amicable relations of these two English-speaking nations. England at that time had many American soldiers on her soil, while others were fighting side by side with Britain's sons in the trenches across the Channel. On this day of July 4, 1918, the Star-

Spangled Banner flew with the Union Jack and American soldiers were fêted with luncheons and banquets. Most important of the functions on that day were the Meeting of Fellowship held in London at Westminster Cathedral and a baseball game between American Army and Navy men, the latter attended by George V, King of England. The Fellowship Meeting was addressed by Lord Bryce, former Ambassador to United States,—the man who, it is said, had done more than any other to cement a firm and inviolate bond between the two nations. Another speaker was Winston Churchill who took as his text the American Declaration of Independence! From the meeting a cablegram was sent to President Wilson and the people of the United States, in which were expressed " Heartfelt greetings on the 142nd anniversary of the Declaration of American Independence."

The American nation had come a long way since that memorable year of 1776. But the common ties of blood and race and speech have kept America and England in close relationship, so that this celebration was not so extraordinary, for bitterness had long since disappeared.

America's Independence Day for the past thirty years has been observed in the north of Denmark. There is, in Jutland, probably the only park of its kind in the world, given over to the celebration of July 4th. Ribild National Bank was built by Danish-born Americans, and in 1909 they began the annual observance with thousands of Danish people. At the ceremonies on July 4, 1934, Ruth Bryan Owen, then Minister to Denmark, dedicated a Lincoln log cabin in the park.

Other nations of the world have their own Independence Days. The Fourteenth of July, or Bastile Day in France, is the birthday of the French Republic. Here is a nation whose independence was won, like America's, because of a love of liberty and freedom. In many ways their Republic is similar to ours; in age, in form of government, and in the character of their freedom-loving people. On the day of the *Fête Nationale* the figure of Liberty is often displayed with the French flag, reminding us of the French gift to America, the Statue of Liberty, which stands in New York harbor.

An Italian holiday corresponding to our Fourth of July is *Festa della Statuto,* a day commemorating the granting of the Italian constitution.

In Canada, there is Dominion Day in observance of the Union of the Dominion of Canada, by Act of Parliament in 1867, from several separate provinces to one unified Dominion.

No person willingly gives up his right to liberty. We in America have been fortunate indeed for we are accustomed to freedom—freedom of speech, freedom of the press, freedom to worship as we please. It has been so directed by our

Constitutional Fathers who said: " We hold these truths to be self-evident, that all men are created equal, that they are endowed by their Creator with certain unalienable Rights, that among these are Life, Liberty and the pursuit of Happiness." Many speeches have been made on this famous paragraph of the Declaration of Independence. In school we study the Declaration, on the Fourth of July we observe its birth, and every day we enjoy its far-reaching results. But let us not take for granted our liberty and our right to happiness. As citizens of these United States—begun as thirteen brave little colonies, united with one purpose, let us, too, adhere to the ideals from which these States have sprung. By loyal patriotism to all those principles bequeathed to us, we can add to the greatness of America and her place in the world.

October 12

COLUMBUS DAY

On a street in Genoa, Italy, there stands a house bearing an inscription on a tablet which, when translated, reads: *No house is more to be honored than this where Christopher Columbus spent his early youth.* It is said that in various accounts of the life of Columbus, sixteen different towns in Italy have been mentioned as his birthplace, although the general belief until very recently has been that the birthplace of the discoverer of America was Genoa. However, in 1930 the famous bibliophile Dr. A. S. W. Rosenbach brought a 400 year old manuscript to this country from London, which is believed to have been written by a friend of Columbus. It gives his birthplace as Milan.

Cristoforo Colombo, as he was named, was born during the Renaissance in 1451. He learned the trade of weaving but when fourteen years of age ran away to sea. On returning home he tried to content himself with helping his father, Domenico. However, after a time he again followed his true love, the sea, that great uncharted world of water which to most people in those days represented only mystery and fear. When still a young boy, Christopher had read the "Travels of Marco Polo" with consuming interest and curiosity, and now that he was grown the dream of his life was to experience for himself some of the daring and colorful adventures of the Venetian traveler—a dream that was realized far more fully than the young boy could have imagined possible, for his name was destined to become one of the most famous of all time.

In the year 1470 Columbus found himself in Portugal, after his ship had been wrecked there, making navigation charts and maps to support his wife and children. But while occupied in the process of making a living, Columbus was dreaming his dream. The brilliant navigator hoped to find a short route to India which would revolutionize trade in the Far East. In spite of the fact that he was practically alone in his belief, Columbus was sure the way existed, for he believed that the earth was round, and he intended navigating the high seas until he found this route. He wanted to make his dream come true, but he needed money. After having tried for financial support in his native Italy and failing, then in Portugal and failing there also, he went to Spain. After many disappointments he gained the whole-hearted support of Queen Isabella, and through her, the financial backing of King Ferdinand for his momentous voyages that were, eventually, to add a whole hemisphere to the known world.

On August 3, 1492, Columbus set out with three small ships— the *Santa Maria,* the *Nina,* and the *Pinta*—and a company of 120 men! On this first voyage into a new world Columbus after four perilous weeks sighted land on October 12th, the day which is now commemorated as Columbus Day. Although he named the land on which they set foot San Salvador, it was what we know as Watling Island, one of the Bahamas. He claimed this land for Spain and, believing it to be a part of India, he returned to Spain where he was greeted with all the honor due a famous traveler. Ferdinand and Isabella were elated. They had entertained little hope that Columbus would be so successful. They, too, believed that the land upon which Columbus had come accidentally was India, and that these brown-skinned men Columbus had brought back for them to see were Indians.

Columbus made three voyages after that. On the second of these he touched upon the shores of South America; on the third he met with little success, either on the voyage or on his return. Then his expeditions were over, for almost immediately after his return to Spain from the last voyage, Queen Isabella died. With the Queen of Spain gone, Columbus fared ill at the hands of the country for which he had claimed the new world. Not only did he never receive any further recognition, but his claims to property rights, which had been promised him, were denied. Lonely, bitter, and disillusioned, Columbus died three years after Isabella on May 20, 1506. He died believing that the land he had found was a short route to the East. Little did he dream that he had played the rôle of Discoverer of America, a twin-continent containing untold riches and the promise of mighty nations of the future!

As with the exact town of his birth, there is some uncertainty concerning the place of Columbus's burial. He had asked to be buried in the spot he loved best, " Espanola "— or Santo Domingo—in the land of his discovery. But as there was no one who cared to carry out Columbus's last wish when he died, he was buried in Seville. However, in 1542 his body, with that of his son, was sent to Santo Domingo as he had so fervently wished. The bodies of father and son were placed in the tombs of the Cathedral where they remained undisturbed until the year 1795 when the Spanish island became a French possession. Spain obtained permission from the French Government to remove them to Cuba, and a coffin was sent to Havana, *supposedly* containing the remains of Columbus. Then in 1877, while the Santo Domingo Cathedral was being repaired, an ancient and crumbling casket was found. On it there was an inscription: " *Discoverer of America—First Admiral*," while on the inside lid was found further proof of its identity: " *Illustrious and noble man, Don Cristobal Colon.*" * Naturally enough, the people of Santo Domingo believed this to be the original casket of Columbus, as it presumably was. Therefore, at the 400th anniversary of Columbus's discovery of America, in 1892, a very handsome monument was erected in the ancient cathedral. Each year on the tenth of September, the anniversary of the finding of the casket, the sides of the giant urn containing the casket are let down so that visitors may see the original coffin in which the famous explorer was laid to rest. This custom is to be enacted annually until 1942 on the 450th anniversary of the Discovery. Meanwhile in Seville, a great monument was built supposedly at the Tomb of Columbus, when his body was purported to have been removed to the Seville Cathedral from Havana. Consequently, two cities claim the honor of being the burying-place of Columbus.

There are many monuments and memorials in the New

* Spanish for Columbus.

World erected to its discoverer. One is the small stone shaft on little Watling Island in the Bahama group of the British West Indies. Its inscription reads: *" On this spot Christopher Columbus first set foot on the soil of the New World."*

Although the continents of the new world were not named for Christopher Columbus, there are cities, towns, rivers and universities honoring his name. Our nation's capital, the District of Columbia, bears his name. Columbus Circle, in New York, where a fine monument stands at the 59th Street entrance to Central Park; and the statue erected in Fairmount Park in Philadelphia in 1876, are only a few of the numerous tributes in his honor. One of the most useful of Columbus memorials is in the Pan-American Building in Washington—the Columbus Memorial Library comprising 90,000 volumes of source material and official documents on the twenty-one American Republics.

Columbus Day was celebrated as a holiday for the first time in 1792 in New York City, on the occasion of the 300th anniversary of the landing of Columbus on American soil. One hundred years later there was a national celebration followed by the Columbian Exposition in Chicago. In 1910 Boston honored October 12th, Massachusetts having made Columbus Day a legal holiday that year. Through the efforts of the Knights of Columbus the day was observed pretty generally throughout the United States and in many

South and Central American countries as well. One by one the states have made Columbus Day a legal holiday, and by 1939 it was such in thirty-five states and Puerto Rico.

In recent years the Central and South American Republics have almost universally celebrated Columbus Day.

For a number of years Spain celebrated Columbus Day in conjunction with *La Fiesta de la Raza,* or Racial Feast Day, on October 12th.

Cuba observes Columbus Day by placing a wreath at the Statue of Columbus at the city hall in Havana. The day is also observed in Haiti, Mexico and Canada.

In 1492 when Columbus sighted land and imagined he had discovered a new way to India, he little thought, nor could he conceive of the immensity of the land of which this was a part! Had he been able to look ahead some four hundred years he might have seen twenty-one republics and great territories, consisting of hundreds of millions of people; great cities, vast agricultural lands and huge forests; earth swelling with rich minerals, and rivers, mountains, lakes and seas, all marking these continents that he had discovered, the most beautiful and productive on the face of the earth. Columbus's achievement, like his dreams, reached out beyond all bounds,—far, far beyond the world in which he lived many years ago, when in " fourteen hundred ninety-two, Columbus sailed the ocean blue."

October 31

HALLOWE'EN

There are still some people, they say, who believe in ghosts!
If you have ever been to a Hallowe'en party in the country
on a dark night, where the scene has been set for attracting
spirits and goblins, and have walked along black corridors
to an equally dark room and felt every second that icy
fingers were about to reach for you, and eerie sounds made
cold chills go up and down your back,—well then, perhaps
you, *too,* have believed in ghosts! And it wasn't a very happy
feeling. Years and years ago, back in the time when Hallowe'en began, most people did believe in spirits and
ghosts,—and witches, fairies, elves, goblins, brownies,

leprechauns, knockers, pookas and bogies! And that was probably not a very comfortable feeling either.

In those days it kept the people very busy indeed around the time of Hallowe'en to keep away the witches, and all these other scary creatures! In Wales they used to say that " On November Eve there is a bogy on every stile." In Scotland a cautious farmer always carried torches about the fields " widdershins " (backward) in order to scare the witches from his property and save his crops. For had he not been told that all the wicked auld dames on that night turned to witches and rode broomsticks, and sported with the devil? It was best to take no chances. Meanwhile the children of Scotland carried jack-o'-lanterns to protect themselves, not unlike our own pumpkin lanterns except that these were made from turnips and were called " bogies."

Burning torches and lanterns and bonfires were, and are still, appropriate to the observance of Hallowe'en. In Wales hilltop fires were an important feature of this night, while the people gathered round and carefully tended the fires until midnight. Then when the last red flames had turned to gray ashes, there was a mad scramble to get down the hill. And woe to the man who was last, for it was said that the devil would get the hindermost!

But how did these customs, so closely bound to Hallowe'en, originate? What was the beginning of this holiday?

Hallowe'en is a day the observance of which is the result of several very old holidays, and it has been kept alive these many years because it was celebrated at a popular time of year for festivals. Most peoples of ancient times observed certain festivals at the turn of the seasons. The Celts and Druids of Ancient Britain, before the invasion of the Romans, had three important ones. These were observed May 1st, June 21st, and October 31st. This last was known as *Samhain,* or Summer's End. It was also the death of the old year, for the Druid calendar celebrated November 1st as the beginning of the New Year. The Druids believed that on the day of *Samhain* all the souls of the dead who had not lived good lives on earth would be compelled to enter into the bodies of animals, while those who deserved it would be given souls of humans. There were many cruel religious rites performed by the Druid priests at this festival of *Samhain,* some of which historians have traced back as far as the Cult of Dionysus of ancient Greece.

With the invasion of Britain by the Romans the Celtic customs, with their heathen and ofttimes unspeakably cruel rites, were changed. A new influence crept into the observance of *Samhain.* It was no longer called *Samhain,* but *Halligan,* and then All Hallows. When gradually the *eve* of All Hallows came to be the time of celebration, the day was called Hallowe'en. The invaders' observance of this day was in honor of the Roman festival *Feralia* which came at the end of October. *Feralia* was a religious day in Rome given over to praying for the dead, and especially honoring those heroes of Rome who had died for their country. This influence, and the Druidistic belief in Reincarnation that was supposed to take place around this time, very likely have given Hallowe'en the atmosphere as we know it today—of ghosts and spirits and the supernatural.

The custom of kindling fires came from the Druid priests and their sacred fires built at their crude stone altars. To the pagans, fire was a symbol of immortality. There has been a belief among all primitive peoples for centuries that fire will frighten away evil spirits, and this probably was the reason for bonfires and torches and the hilltop fires of Hallowe'en.

For hundreds of years in a town in Somerset, England, the children have paraded the streets on the last Thursday in October carrying small candle lanterns made from man-golds. They call them " punkies."

There is an old Irish legend concerning the origin of jack-o'-lanterns: because of his stinginess, a man named Jack was kept out of heaven and was not allowed to enter hell because of the jokes he played on the devil. His only recourse was to roam the earth, and he was condemned to do just that until Judgment Day, carrying a lantern.

The popularity of telling fortunes on Hallowe'en probably came from the fact that this was the Celtic New Year, and the first day of the new year has always been considered a good time to tell fortunes. The Irish and Scotch had all sorts of ways of foretelling the future. Many of these dealt with a girl's finding out who her husband was to be. If she made a cake of flour, salt and soot, ate it and went to bed, the man who came to her in her dream offering her a drink of water was the man she was to marry! Another method was to throw a ball of yarn into the outside bake oven. Holding fast to one end, the girl was supposed to wind it in slowly until she felt it being held by someone (supposedly her true love), then she would call: "Wha'hauds?" And if she were lucky, the name of her future husband would come in to her from the kiln-pot. A good way for a man to see his future mate was to sow hempseed.

> *Hempseed, I saw thee,*
> *Hempseed, I saw thee;*
> *And her that is to be my true love,*
> *Come after me and pou thee.*

Throwing apple parings over the left shoulder is still done on Hallowe'en today as it was then, swinging the unbroken paring over the head three times before it drops to spell the initial of the beloved.

Nuts are used in many places to foretell the future on Hallowe'en; indeed, in some parts of northern England Hallowe'en has been called Nutcrack Night. Parties gather before the fire on this chill autumn night to tell stories— tales of ghosts probably, prognosticating the future with the nuts as they roast them. Those that burn bright upon being thrown into the fire supposedly bring good luck and prosperity to the person who threw them. If a young man and a maid each threw a nut into the flame and they burned together, that meant the two would be married!

In England girls gathered yarrow and put it under their pillows hoping to see the vision of their future husbands in their dreams; while a youth who wanted to know the identity of his future wife could put nine grains of oats in his mouth and walk abroad until he heard her name spoken!

A description of the activities of an Irish household on Hallowe'en in the early nineteenth century gives us an idea of the importance of these customs to all members of the family.

" The buxom good wife was regaling her friends with merry lamb's-wool (punch) while her lively children and their young guests indulged in the usual superstitions and quaint customs of All Hallow Eve. Three of the eldest lasses were lurking in a dark corner busily employed in kneading a cake with their left thumbs. Not a sound escaped from their clenched lips; the work proceeded in mute solemnity; a single word would have broken the charm and destroyed their ardent hopes of beholding their future husbands in their dreams after having partaken of the mystic ' dumb-cake.' "

Hallowe'en in Ireland, even to this day, is celebrated by a dinner with special foods not served at any other time of the year. The writer just quoted tells of a Hallowe'en dinner consisting of " laughing potatoes," turkey, caulcannon, and apple pies. The caulcannon was a very special Hallowe'en dish made from mashed potatoes, parsnips, and chopped onions into which had been placed the following: *a ring,* designating marriage; *a doll,* predicting children to come; *a thimble,* meaning the recipient would be an old maid; and *a coin,* standing for wealth. Today this same custom is often carried out at Hallowe'en parties, the objects for foretelling the future of those who receive them being baked in a cake.

Cabbages have played a rôle in Hallowe'en customs on the British Isles. In Scotland young women determined the appearance of the men they would marry by drawing, blindfolded, cabbages from the garden. The close white heads meant an old husband, while an open green head meant a young man! Then his disposition could be determined by the sweetness of the stem's taste. It was said that a cabbage hung over the door would give a much better clue to the man's identity, for the first man's name spoken by anyone who entered would be the Christian name of the future husband! Children placed cabbages before the door believing that a baby sister or brother would come to the house before the year was out.

It was bad luck to eat blackberries or sloes on *any* day except Hallowe'en, or so it was believed in some sections of England.

There was so much superstition connected with the happenings of Hallowe'en in old Scotland that a child born on this day was said to have supernatural powers. As Sir Walter Scott pointed out in *The Monastery*, " It's weel kenn'd she was born on Hallowe'en whiles see mair than ither folk."

Hallowe'en in Queen Elizabeth's time was a real holiday, with shops closed and lots of parties and fireworks and parades! Even so long ago as that there was ducking for apples at parties, and other Hallowe'en games which are still played today.

The custom of masquerading on Hallowe'en probably derived from mummers in the English parades and *guizarts* in Scotland who dressed in queer costumes and went about chanting rhymes.

Boys and young men of Syria dress up in funny clothes

and go from house to house on Hallowe'en, pretty much as we do here in America, and they are received with cakes and a special drink flavored with anise.

In modern Ireland people eat sowans on Hallowe'en; also barmbrack, a kind of bread containing raisins and currants. Caulcannon is still eaten there too, as the feature dish of a Hallowe'en meal.

While Hallowe'en in America lacks the superstitious character of the Old World holiday, it does, nevertheless, retain many of the old customs such as masquerading, visiting from house to house, bobbing for apples, and eating the ever-popular apples and nuts of the autumn season. It is now chiefly a holiday for the children, though grown people like to entertain on Hallowe'en, too. School parties are the custom now, especially for the children of the lower grades, and on the afternoon of Hallowe'en in the average American town these children on their way home can be seen—little Indians and Chinese and gypsies—carrying a small orange-colored packet of nuts and candy-corn and perhaps an apple from the school party.

In many towns there are parades on Hallowe'en in which the school children can take part, with prizes offered for the best costumes. But aside from the parades and parties of Hallowe'en, it is a great evening for the children, for it gives them freedom for fun and pranks that no other holiday permits. If a gate disappears on Hallowe'en and is found next day hanging from the branch of a tree, that was the witches at their tricks! If the doorbell rings or there is a tick-tack at the window, it's spooks! And there's the fun of being disguised so that even the next-door neighbor has a hard time recognizing these strange-looking people who have come to the front door,—to say nothing of the ginger cookies, apples, pears, nuts, popcorn, peanuts and candy that disappear like magic every time they are passed round! In the olden days this may have been an important holiday for grown-ups, but today it is a time for the boys and girls, one of the happiest holidays of the whole year and one not likely soon to disappear.

November 1

ALL SAINTS' and ALL SOULS'

Hallowe'en is also the Eve of All Saints' Day, and its celebration in some countries coincides with the customs

of All Saints'. November 2d is All Souls' Day, and with
the three days coming one right after the other—Hallowe'en, All Saints', and All Souls'—some of the customs
have much in common. Since the origin of Hallowe'en
was the Roman Feralia, a time for praying for the dead, and
All Souls' is a day devoted to that purpose, there is at least
a slight similarity between the two days. In Wales the Eve
of All Saints' (Hallowe'en) is spent in telling fortunes,
trying to determine the future; while twenty-four hours later
on the Eve of All Souls' the minds of the people have
turned to the dead. On the Eve of All Saints' the peasants
of Wales believed that they could, by peeping through the
keyhole of the church door, see the apparitions of those
who would pass on to the next world in the year to come.
On the Eve of All Souls' they were praying for the souls
of those who had already departed. There and in some parts
of England they have at this time what they call a soul-cake,
because in years gone by it was customary to give a cake
in return for prayers for the dead.

> *Soul! Soul! for a soul-cake!*
> *I pray, good misses, a soul-cake!*
> *An apple or pear, a plum or a cherry,*
> *Any good thing to make us merry,*
> *One for Peter, two for Paul,*
> *Three for Him who made us all.*

So the carollers sang on the Eve of All Souls' as they went about from farmhouse to farmhouse, "souling." Thought to bring good fortune, some people kept soul-cakes in the house from year to year. In Yorkshire this was known as Cake Night for it was the custom there for the mother of the family to bake a special seed cake for every member of the family.

Portuguese children on All Souls' receive sugar-cakes made of herbs, sugar and cinnamon as a reward for their songs.

In France there is a combined celebration of All Saints' and All Souls'. On the day before All Saints' (Hallowe'en) children go about begging flowers to put in the cemeteries. There is a very distinct difference, however, in the celebration of the two days. On All Saints' there are flowers and lighted candles in the churches, and the music is that of rejoicing. But on All Souls' the atmosphere changes to one of great solemnity. Draped with black the church assumes a funereal aspect. The French are very respectful of the dead on All Souls'; the cemeteries are crowded with men, women and children who are busy decorating the graves of their departed.

Many European people not only decorate the graves with flowers and wreaths, but they also leave gifts there for the souls of the dead. In Lithuania great baskets of food are taken to the cemetery where the people partake of the feast of good things, leaving for the departed that food which was not eaten by the living!

The Mexicans observe a three-day All Souls', from October 30th to November 2d. The last day is the Day of the Dead, and from sunrise until the end of the day the cemeteries are crowded. Here, too, they carry great amounts of food to the cemetery, and a good time is had by all, for the Mexicans make a holiday of this day, devoting it to the children, those living and those departed. Among the eatables there is always "Dead Men's Bread," candied pumpkin and chocolate, and sweets made in the shape of skulls and coffins! When they are ready to leave they always remember to leave sweets for the dead.

There is a belief among the Polish people that the Lord comes to the cemeteries on All Souls' to count the souls of those fortunate ones who have been saved.

Chinese and Japanese calendars include a festival corresponding to the occidental All Souls'; in China it is called the Festival of the Unforgotten Dead; in Japan it is the Feast of Lanterns, celebrated from July 13th to 15th. After the souls have feasted for a period of three days they are content to pass on to the world beyond, and are lighted on their way by lanterns.

All Saints' Day in our own country is observed in the

Roman Catholic, Greek Catholic, and the Protestant Episcopal churches. In the State of Louisiana it is a legal holiday. The Roman Catholic churches also observe All Souls' Day.

November 11

ARMISTICE DAY

This holiday is commemorative of the Armistice signed between the combatants of the First World War. After four years of terrific struggle—1914 to 1918—in which almost every nation of the world had become involved, a truce was signed. For three days in the Forest of Compiègne, a peace treaty was discussed between Marshal Foch and representatives of the despairing German Government. At last the terms were agreed upon, and at five o'clock in the morning the Armistice was signed, with orders for all hostilities to cease at eleven A. M. that day.

The time: eleven o'clock on the eleventh day of the eleventh month in 1918. That was the beginning of Armistice Day, now a legal holiday in the United States.

That day in New York, and in all the length and breadth
of America, in the British Isles, in Italy, and especially in
France where most of the fighting had taken place, was a
day of untold joy! Peace had come, peace at last after four
awful years of unspeakable fighting on land, in the air, and
at sea. Peace! That was all that mattered, and as the bells
rang out and whistles blew and people shouted and wept
and sang for joy, a new holiday was born. What the day
was to mean in the future was no concern at this time of
precious victory. The realization of the moment was of a
cessation of fighting, silence on the battlefields, an empty-
ing of the trenches, of crowds thronging the streets and
every heart overflowing with gladness!

On the night of the Armistice crowds grew dense while
the streets of European cities, darkened for so long, were
once more blazing with lights. In Paris the cafés overflowed with people who wished to stay up all night to
discuss the wonderful turn of events. In London thousands
of people pushed their way to Number 10 Downing Street
and sang, "Lloyd George, Lloyd George, oh he's a jolly
good fellow"—while 20,000 people pressed, singing and
cheering, against the palace where the Royal Family came
out upon the balcony to rejoice with them. In New York
crowds went wild; bands played; a tremendous shower of
paper littered the streets and fell like snow upon thousands

of hysterically happy Americans. This was the first Armistice Day.

All modern history books give full accounts of the World War, its cause and effects. At the present time a second European War is being waged between Germany and the Allies, and the Armistice that was signed on November 11, 1918, seems suddenly to have changed its meaning, though its importance in the world struggle of the democracies must not be minimized. However, to explain the meaning of the holiday and its celebration, it is not necessary for us to go into the history of the War.

The first anniversary of the Armistice, in 1919, found the world still in the throes of reconstruction and rehabilitation after the chaos of battle, with innumerable problems, international and internal, that would take years to solve.

The following year Armistice Day was observed in France and in England by the impressive ceremony of the burial of an Unknown Soldier by both nations. France disinterred an unidentified *poilu* from among her 1,357,800 dead, placing him with reverence and sadness in a sarcophagus in the *Arc de Triomphe*, Paris. A perpetual flame burning there since that time honors the one who represents all of the French soldiers who fell in the World War.

On that same day in London a similar ceremony took place at famous Westminster Abbey. From the graves of nearly one million men Britain honored one,—an Unknown Soldier—as the symbol of all who had given their lives for their country. Thus another famous tomb took its place in the Abbey among a legion of English kings and queens. For one week after November 11th the grave was left open while thousands filed by in an almost continuous line. On the day that the tomb was closed a maple leaf arrived from a Canadian comrade who had fought for the Motherland, and it was placed in the sarcophagus of the Unknown Soldier.

Following the custom of France and England, America on the next Armistice Day, November 11, 1921, buried her Unknown Soldier. There were four American cemeteries in France filled with white crosses, showing the last resting places of thousands of our men who had crossed the sea and fought valiantly at the Front, only to perish. In the National Cemetery at Arlington thousands more lay buried. From France an American soldier was to be brought to Arlington, one of the many whose graves were marked *Unknown*. Because of the cruelty of war many soldiers had necessarily to be buried without ever having been identified. The United States would choose one of these nameless lads to symbolize the American youths who had fallen.

From each of the American cemeteries,—Belleau, Bony, Romagne, and Thiancourt—a body was disinterred. The four coffins were taken to the City Hall in Chalon-sur-Marne and placed in a flag-draped room. Then, while the band played the sad notes of a funeral dirge, a sergeant of the Fifty-Ninth Infantry placed a bouquet of white roses on one of the four coffins. The coffin upon which the white roses lay was placed in a casket marked with this inscription: "*An unknown American soldier who gave his life in the great war.*"

In this manner was the identity of the soldier concealed. Arriving in Washington on November 9th, the body remained lying in state in the rotunda of the Capitol Building, where for three days the respect and reverence of the American people were shown in the steady stream of persons who passed by. On Armistice Day countless wreaths were placed about the casket. From all over the nation and from many foreign countries came flowers and messages. From King George of Britain, written by his own hand, came these words:

" As unknown and yet well known, as dying, and behold, we live."

Armistice Day was officially made a holiday in that year when the Unknown Soldier was buried. President Harding and Secretary of War Weeks were the speakers at the ceremony at Arlington. On that day in England, General Pershing had decorated the grave of the British Unknown

Soldier at Westminster Abbey with the American Congressional Medal of Honor.

Until 1938 Armistice Day was a national holiday by annual proclamation of the President of the United States. On June 4, 1926, a Resolution in Congress had provided: " That the President of the United States is requested to issue a proclamation calling upon the officials to display the flag of the United States on all Government buildings on November 11th and inviting the people of the United States to observe the day in schools and churches, or other suitable places, with appropriate ceremonies expressive of our gratitude for peace and our desire for the continuance of friendly relations with all other peoples." Then by an act of Congress approved May 13, 1938, Armistice Day was made a legal holiday " to be dedicated to the cause of world peace . . ." and continuing, " Whereas, It is fitting at this time of world unrest that November 11, 1938, the twentieth anniversary of the armistice, should be observed with suitable ceremonies manifesting our belief that peace can be attained only by non-aggression and can be made enduring only by respect for the rights of others and good-will among the nations of the world."

Churches throughout America observe the Sunday preceding Armistice Day in dedication to Peace and to honor the heroes of the World War. At eleven o'clock on the morning of November 11th, the true anniversary of the Armistice, a two-minute silence is observed by the people of this nation, and is also held at that time in England. The " Great Silence " was originated by one Edward George Honey, an Australian journalist who died in 1922. The ceremony at Arlington National Cemetery on Armistice Day, when a wreath is placed on the Tomb of the Unknown Soldier, is duplicated almost exactly in London at Westminster Abbey and in Paris at the *Arc de Triomphe.* England and France as well as America have observed Armistice Day annually. In England it has come to be known as Remembrance Day. In France, where it is *Jour de l'Armistice,* every town and village has cause to remember the Armistice and the events leading up to it.

The observance of Armistice Day in the United States of America has for over twenty years emphasized peace and goodwill among nations. Apparently all other countries were of the same mind. Peace conferences were held, the League of Nations was formed and functioned successfully for years; the world even disarmed. But distrust on the part of nations toward each other, acts of aggression by European powers, and cautious but certain steps toward world armament once more filled the peoples of the world with fear and unrest. Finally, on September 3, 1939, a state of war was declared to exist between England and Germany and

France and Germany as a result of the German invasion of Poland on September 1st. To us here in America, the state of war in Europe gives new meaning to Armistice Day. With all the sanity and intelligence and enthusiasm of which we are capable, then, we should make this a day of Peace,—Peace and Remembrance. Remembering the horrors of the days and years that preceded the Armistice, and the relief and joy that came after, let us cling tenaciously to that state of existence which keeps us close to all that makes life worth while, and shun forever those things that lead to war. Let us, if we can, by the grace of God, continue in the peace that began on that first Armistice Day in the French Forest of Compiègne, when guns ceased firing.

THANKSGIVING DAY

" Over the river, and through the woods, to Grandmother's house we go! " That's the song we used to sing on Thanksgiving Day, and that is what we used to do. Nearly everyone who had a grandmother went to her house for a big family gathering on Thanksgiving Day and, more important to the children, a big family dinner! Turkey, cranberry sauce, mashed turnips and giblet gravy, pumpkin pies and apples and nuts, and plenty of everything! Then the song goes: " The horse knows the way to carry the sleigh o'er the white and drifting snow! " Bells jangling, children shouting from the straw-filled body of the sleigh, blankets pulled up to chins by mittened hands; father guiding the

horses and mother beside him, anxious to arrive in time
for her to help with the big dinner. Then the fun of unload-
ing, rushing to get into the warm kitchen where the odors
of a delicious feast were almost overpowering to hungry
senses! To describe the way the turkey tasted, that browned
handsome bird just bursting with chestnut filling and so big
he covered Grandma's huge white platter from edge to
edge, would only be doing an injustice to the turkey! Yes,
the memories of Thanksgiving Day at Grandmother's are
sweet to many.

Let us go back to the first Thanksgiving Day in America.
It was the year 1621 and the date was December 13th.
That day had been set in the Plymouth Colony by Governor
Bradford as a time for being thankful and showing gratitude to Almighty God for the bounties received in this
land of hardship and struggle. Elder Brewster conducted
the Thanksgiving church service among the loyal band of
fifty-five in the Plymouth settlement. Then there was a rare
feast for these people who had perforce to be so sparing
with food. Governor Bradford had appointed four of the
best marksmen to go hunting and bring back enough food
for a feast. They had been unusually successful, having
brought back to the settlement many wild turkeys and quails.
The Pilgrims were joined at their feast by King Massasoit
and ninety Indian braves who presented Governor Bradford

with the welcome gift of five deer. History tells us that this first Thanksgiving lasted for three days.

It is quite probable that the idea for a Thanksgiving Day presented itself to the pilgrims through any one or all of three sources. First, the English had, in the course of history, observed various days of Thanksgiving from time to time. Guy Fawkes Day in that country had originally been a day of thanks proclaimed " in grateful deliverance " of the uncovering of the famous Gunpowder Plot in 1605, a plot to blow up Parliament on November 5th of that year and discovered in time to avert the disaster. Although Guy Fawkes Day was dropped from the British calendar in 1833, it is still observed to some degree in England, Australia and some other colonies. Aside from this, other days of Thanksgiving, proclaimed by the ruling monarchs of England and set aside as days of gratitude for some victory or other, had been observed from time to time.

Another influence that cannot be ignored emanated from Holland. It will be remembered that the Pilgrims in fleeing from England had found refuge with the Dutch for several years before deciding to brave the hardships they later encountered on the wild, strange shores of America. This band of men, women and children so earnestly seeking religious freedom was happy in Holland and while making their homes with the peace-loving Hollanders, they probably acquired the custom of observing their holidays, for in Holland there was a Thanksgiving Day,—in remembrance of Holland's victory over Spain in the year 1575. The Dutch Thanksgiving was observed in October.

The third possibility as a reminder to the Puritans to establish a Thanksgiving Day was the influence of the Indians. King Massasoit was friendly toward the Pilgrim Fathers and it is not hard to imagine that the Indian custom of celebrating " thanksgiving " days appealed to the devout founders of New England. From histories of the American Indians and their customs we know that most if not all of the tribes observed times of thanksgiving.

At any rate, the Puritan settlers of New England liked the idea of a Thanksgiving Day because of the nature of the holiday. It was a time set apart by them for giving thanks for all the good things they had received during the year, especially for the harvest. The Puritans both in America and England frowned upon Christmas because of the boisterous type of celebration in vogue at that time. So the new holiday seemed superior. While Christmas was condemned as sinful and its celebration was absolutely forbidden in the New England colonies, Thanksgiving was faithfully observed. In fact, a law was passed to the effect that a fine of five shillings be imposed on those who did any " servile labour or worke " on Thanksgiving Day!

But the American Thanksgiving as a holiday had no established permanence for more than two hundred years after its first celebration. During the Revolution there were eight different days of Thanksgiving appointed by Continental Congress as days of gratefulness for victorious battles in the war. The first move to set aside a national holiday in which the whole country might take part did not come until 1789, when President Washington designated November 26th of that year as a national Thanksgiving Day. But unity, even in the matter of holidays, was difficult at that time, transportation and communication being what they were! After 1795 there wasn't another national Thanksgiving Day until the Civil War when, in 1862, Abraham Lincoln called on the nation to give thanks for victories in the War.

And now we come to the great defender and promulgator of Thanksgiving, Mrs. Sarah Hale. Editor of *Gody's Lady's Book,* Mrs. Hale had for years been rousing interest in a Thanksgiving that should be a truly national holiday—equal in importance to the Fourth of July! This sincere and persevering woman made herself personally responsible for seeing that *all* the states should observe the day. She wrote to the Governors urging their support, and thousands of letters from her pen went to those who could help along the cause. Having persistently waged her campaign for many years, she finally wrote to President Lincoln and sent him a copy of George Washington's proclamation in which he had asked the people to observe the day (November 26, 1789) "to the service of that Great and Glorious Being Who is the beneficent author of all the good that was, that is, or that will be."

Sarah Hale's reward came when President Lincoln's proclamation in 1862 made the last Thursday in November an annual national holiday! And today Thanksgiving is a legal holiday in every state, territory and possession of the United States. The custom since Lincoln's time, by tradition, has been for the President to proclaim the holiday for the District of Columbia and the Territories and Possessions of the United States, and for the Governors of the states to follow suit by proclaiming the holiday for their respective states. On the Sunday preceding Thanksgiving Day, the President's Proclamation is read from pulpits in churches all over the nation.

In his Proclamation of 1938 Franklin D. Roosevelt after citing the examples set by Washington and Lincoln in proclaiming days of thanksgiving for the nation said:

"Thus from our earliest recorded history, Americans have thanked God for their blessings. In our deepest natures, in our very souls, we, like all mankind, since the earliest origin of mankind, turn to God in time of happiness. ' In

God we trust.' " His Proclamation of August 15, 1939, called upon the nation to observe Thanksgiving on the third Thursday in November of that year. This deviation from the usual date continued in 1940 and 1941.

Thanksgiving Day is probably more of a family holiday than any other on our calendar. It is a time when all who can possibly do so go home. Schools and colleges usually give students a vacation of several days. In every town and city in America there are early morning church services, and in a great many places there are important football games.

Children in some cities dress up—paint themselves like Indians or mask as they do on Hallowe'en, and beg pennies from people on the street. In New York City it isn't unusual to be accosted on the street corner by them with the frank plea for pennies. " Anything for Thanksgiving? " they ask. This custom is thought to be a relic of the old Guy Fawkes Day in England.

Since ancient times there have been holidays and festivals similar to our Thanksgiving. Among the Israelites certain feast days were set apart for giving thanks. The Greeks celebrated nine days of thanksgiving for the harvest in their Feast of Demeter. Similar was the Feast of Cerelia in Rome. The Druids of Ancient Britain observed a harvest festival in November, while the early English Harvest Home was an important time of the year among the country people.

The Scotch celebrate the Kern when the harvest is taken in, and in late September there used to be harvest festivals among the Czecho-Slovakians, Poles and Lithuanians, while in Russia the harvest festival was one of the most important of the whole year. Famous at the festival of the Russians was the *khorovod,* a dance expressing the entire routine of the harvest. At that time a wreath from the year before, made from wheat, oats, barley, and rye, with customary ritual was removed from the side of the house and a new one put in its place, while the girls and boys chanted these words: " Good luck, good luck to the house."

A harvest feast called *Höst Gilde* is celebrated in Norway when the harvest has been taken in for the year.

The Siamese have a " Swing Festival " which is observed annually to show gratitude for bounties received.

In Canada Thanksgiving Day is celebrated annually, usually on the last Thursday of October.

In certain sections of Pennsylvania there is a sect known as the Schwenkfelders—so-called from their founder, Caspar von Schwenkfelder, a follower of John Huss in the early sixteenth century—who have a Thanksgiving Day peculiar to themselves on September 24th. It commemorates their landing in Philadelphia in 1724 on that date, when they came seeking religious liberty just as the Pilgrim fathers had done a hundred years earlier.

Returning once more to the first Thanksgiving Day in America, it may seem strange to us now living on this continent in the midst of all the comforts the Pilgrims lacked, that they who fought every hardship for existence should have found something to be thankful for. But the Pilgrim fathers were grateful for the same things for which the Indians thanked their gods,—tall waving corn in the fields, pumpkins on the vine, potatoes, turkey, deer, and for the sunshine and rain that brought the harvest, and for the forests that yielded wood for protection and warmth. If they could be thankful for the bare necessities of life, we who have so much have good cause to celebrate Thanksgiving Day. And while being grateful, let us not forget to think of those patient, persistent and hard-headed colonists who braved the unbroken land of a new continent to establish a land of freedom for their children, their children's children, and for you and me.

December 25

CHRISTMAS

" And she brought forth her first-born son, and wrapped him in swaddling clothes, and laid him in a manger; because there was no room for them in the inn.

And there were in the same country shepherds abiding in the field, keeping watch over their flock by night.

And, lo, the angel of the Lord came upon them, and the glory of the Lord shone round about them: and they were sore afraid.

And the angel said unto them, Fear not: for, behold, I bring you good tidings of great joy, which shall be to all people.

For unto you is born this day in the city of David a Saviour, which is Christ the Lord."   *St. Luke 2: 7–11.*

In the little town of Bethlehem, Judea, birthplace of David the king, Jesus was born of Mary nearly two thousand years ago. That was the first Christmas.

There is no other day of the year like Christmas. In every Christian country of the world it is the most important and meaningful holiday of the whole calendar year. Commemorative of the birth of Christ it is also the anniversary of a new age, the era of Christianity. For on that day there came into the world a Great Teacher who was to bring light to countless millions, influencing whole nations and races of men. His birth is celebrated annually from one end of the world to the other in churches and great cathedrals, and in the homes and hearts of the people.

Strangely enough, the date of Christ's birth is not known with certainty. As a matter of fact, it was not until 354 years after His birth that December 25th was first observed as His birthday. Some believed the true date to be November 17th, others claimed it was March 28th, but since the year 354 when Bishop Liberius of Rome started to observe Christmas on December 25th, that date has been permanent.

Although the true meaning of Christmas is its religious observance, there are customs associated with this holiday's celebration that have been grafted on from pagan times; ancient customs that have survived the age in which they were born through continuous practice by the people. And because they are very old, these customs have come to the Christmas festival from many different nations. From Ancient Rome the Saturnalia contributed; from the Druids of Western Europe and Celtic Britain, from the Ancient Germans, Scandinavia, and Persia, customs were borrowed for the new festival, the Birthday of Christ. Either directly or indirectly, customs from the Roman, Persian, Norse, Hebrew, Gothic, and Anglo-Saxon worlds gradually lent their influence to the celebration of Christmas.

It is true that, for many years, the holy day was kept as a church festival only, with reverent ceremonies in early Christian churches and none of the outside influences just mentioned. But there came a time when holidays and holy days were celebrated with intense enthusiasm by the peasant classes of England, Ireland, Scotland, and many nations of the continent. Those were the days when May Day was at its height in Merrie England, and Hallowe'en in Ireland and Scotland was an important occasion. From the distinctly religious character of Christmas, the pendulum swung the other way, and in the early seventeenth century the holiday had become so rowdy and boisterous that it had to be abolished by law! This was during the time of the Puritans, for, with their wholly restrained way of living, they frowned upon all holidays, considering them worldly and frivolous. In 1643 while the Puritans were in power, Parliament abolished Christmas, Easter, and Whitsuntide from the calendar and made their recognition unlawful. Likewise in the New England colonies of America the Puritan influence was being felt. In the Massachusetts Bay Colony a law was passed making the observance of Christmas a penal offense. That was in 1659 and the result was rather sad for New England, for so deeply imbedded in the minds of the stern Puritan fathers had this prejudice been that more than a hundred years passed before the day was celebrated to any extent. About the time of the Civil War Massachusetts began to observe some of the Christmas traditions of the rest of the country.

Prior to the " relapse " which the holiday suffered at the time of the Puritans, there were years of joyful Christmas celebrations in England that form a part of English tradition. The first keeping of Christmas on record in England was in the year 521 when King Arthur took over the city of York with a real celebration there in the truly Christian manner, banishing heathen rites that reflected the still-persistent Roman Saturnalia. From an ancient book published in 1608 there is an account of Christmas as it was celebrated by a certain rich squire of the time, showing that period's enthusiasm for the holiday:

"At a Christmas time, when great logs furnish the hall fire,— when brawne is in season, and, indeede, all reveling is regarded, this gallant knight kept open house for all commers, where beefe, beere, and bread was no niggard. Amongst all the pleasures provided, a noyse of minstrells and a Lincolnshire bagpipe was prepared—the minstrells for the great chamber, the bagpipe for the hall—the minstrells to serve up the knights meate, and the bagpipe for the common dauncing."

Minstrels were used in the court of the king. Those mentioned above were probably wandering minstrels, a group of men who traveled from place to place making music, and of course at Christmas time they were more than welcome in the big houses that overflowed with guests and the joyful spirit of the season! Known as the Christmas waites, there were usually four or five men who carried bagpipes and drum, or fiddle, flageolet and harp, which they employed with plenty of vigor in all the tunes they knew. Celebrations were not confined to one or two days. In the great houses of the country squires they were apt to last from Christmas to Candlemas, a period of five weeks. From Christmas to Twelfth Night was a time of continuous feasting, music and dancing, frolicking and fun—a veritable carnival. It was about this time that the Lord of Misrule came into being; at this time, too, that Christmas lost its religious character and at the same time fell out of favor with the Puritans.

The Lord of Misrule was a strange stepchild of Christmas, seeming to us, as to the Puritans of that time, far removed in spirit from the celebration of Christ's birthday.

In the time of Queen Elizabeth the Lord of Misrule was at the height of his popularity. Chosen by the people to head the Christmas festivities, he in turn chose a Fool and a Jester as his two chief assistants. These three made plans for the celebrations, heading the Mummers and planning the parades. Misrule it was, for law and order were forgotten by that noisy, boisterous, lawless crowd that took possession of the town at this time. All the true significance of Christmas was lost in this queer unrestrained way of celebrating. We cannot wonder at the Puritans' abhorrence of the day.

In spite of this period when the holiday for a time ceased to be celebrated, England was to find Christmas once more. Years later a famous English writer was to make the English Yuletide world-famous. Charles Dickens' immortal "Christmas Carol" is probably more familiar to the world today than any other Christmas lore with the exception of the story of the Nativity.

Today no holiday on the calendar is so dear to the heart of an Englishman as Christmas. The English children hang up their stockings just as the American children do. The house is decorated with holly and mistletoe from Christmas to Candlemas, and of course there is always a Christmas tree! There the tree is kept in a tub of earth so that it may be replanted, a custom that is just beginning to come to the attention of others as much better than letting the evergreen wither and die and be thrown on the ash heap,—the tragedy of Andersen's "Fir-Tree." The idea of a living Christmas tree seems more in keeping with the Yuletide spirit.

What would Christmas be without a Santa Claus? That indispensable and genial character who *is* Christmas to millions of little children all over the world has come into being through tradition that has grown with the centuries. His story is an interesting one. Yes, indeed, there *was* a real Santa Claus!

St. Nicholas, or *San Nicholaus* as it is pronounced in several foreign tongues, of which Santa Claus is a contraction, was a saint whose feast day is December 6th. That is why in Holland and Belgium December 6th is the day when boys and girls receive their gifts from him instead of on Christmas Day.

Nicholas was born at the close of the third century in Lycia, Asia Minor. Later he became Bishop of Myra and gained distinction as a member of the Council of Nicea, in the year 325. The good Bishop was famed for his kind heart. A story is told of his helping three maidens who were without suitors. It is said that he filled three purses with gold and threw them into the homes of the young women, and soon after, with such dowries, they were married. After that, any unexpected gift was attributed to Nicholas.

Gradually, through the years, he came to be known as the patron Saint of children. In the town of Bari, Italy, where St. Nicholas is buried, they do not associate him with Christmas. His day is celebrated there not in December but on May 7th because that was the day, in 1807, on which his remains were brought from Asia Minor and buried at Bari. Pilgrimages are made to the beautiful temple built there in his honor.

St. Nicholas seems to have been adopted first by Holland as the patron Saint of Christmas; today, in some form, his name is familiar to children of nations scattered over the entire world. True, he is not always known as St. Nicholas or even as Santa Claus, but he is none the less real to the children for all that. Father Christmas, *Kris Kringle, Pelz-nickel, Yule Tomten, La Befana, Petit Noel, Christkindli,—* all these are Santa Claus to the little ones of some land, extremely important to a Christmas celebration.

The legend that Santa Claus comes down the chimney belongs to the Norsemen. They had a goddess Hertha appearing in the fireplace to bring good fortune to the house. From them also came the custom of burning the Yule log. The *Juul* was burnt annually in honor of the god Thor. So well-established had the custom become that, in England, in the days of Christmas waites, boar's head dinners and mutton-pies, the Yule log was the most important feature of the occasion. With a great deal of ceremony it was brought in and placed in the huge fireplace in the great center hall where the fire was started with a bit of the old Yule log from the year before. The English still have their Yule log. In Serbia great importance is attached to the burning of the *Badnyak,* when certain significant rituals are performed that are thought to bring good fortune upon the house.

The giving of gifts at the Christmas season is reminiscent of the Wise Men who brought gifts to the Holy Child. " And when they were come into the house, they saw the young child with Mary his mother, and fell down, and worshipped him: and when they had opened their treasures, they presented unto him gifts; gold, and frankincense, and myrrh."

In France instead of hanging up their stockings the boys and girls put out their shoes for the *Petit Jesu* to fill. This custom started long ago when children placed their shoes, filled with oats, on the doorstep for the camels of the three Wise Men that they might eat while on their journey to Bethlehem. If they had been good children they found that the Wise Men had left gifts in their shoes. In Spain and Mexico, and Latin American countries, children place their shoes at the foot of the bed or on the balcony on the Eve of Epiphany, January sixth, for that is the time the Wise Men were supposed to have been on their journey to visit the Christ Child.

One of the most beautiful customs of the Birthday of Christ is the enactment of the Nativity. From the most ceremonious rituals on midnight of Christmas Eve in the world's largest and most beautiful cathedral, St. Peter's in Rome, where the Pope with his Guard of Honor and the Bishops and Cardinals take part, down to the tiniest miniature Bethlehem arranged under a Christmas tree, all are representative of that holy night when Christ was born. In an Italian household there is the *Presepio,* dear to the heart of every member of the family. *Presepio* is the Italian word for stable but it is now used to designate the scene of the Nativity with its shepherds, camels and sheep, the three Wise Men, the figures of Mary and Joseph, and a little manger containing the tiny figure of the *Bambino,* the Holy Infant. In our own country we have a custom of arranging little villages, with trees, and houses and people under the Christmas tree. The Moravians of Pennsylvania have their *Putz* at Christmas. The *Putz* is similar to the Italian *Presepio* except that it is always under or near a tree with a bright star suspended above it, some of them taking up half a room. The tiny figures of the *Putz* are saved from year to year and for generations, endeared to the family that owns them. A moss-covered hillside on which sheep are grazing, a tiny shepherd looking up at the bright star, and, in a sequestered part of the hillside, a cave-like stable holding its precious burden, with Mary and Joseph nearby, and the three Wise Men kneeling at the door,—all these create an impression of realism to the beholder. The first *Putz* this writer ever saw was in Nazareth, Pennsylvania. One such as has just been described. The only light in the room came from the gleaming star hanging above, and as we looked down on the little Judean scene, the mother of that household related in soft tones the story of the First Christmas.

Every Christmas season in Mexico brings the *Posadas,* an enactment of the Nativity that lasts for nine nights. Nine families take part, and each night the group meets in a different house. A procession starts the *Posada* led by two children carrying images of Mary and Joseph. Followed by family, guests and servants, they wander from room to room chanting the Litany of Loretto. At the door of each room they beg for admittance and are refused. But in the last room they are admitted, and here there is an altar representing the scene of the Nativity with tiny figures and an empty manger in the stable. On the first night the figures of Mary and Joseph are placed in the stable, but the manger remains empty until the last *Posada* on Christmas Eve.

In Bagdad there is a custom of burning dried thorns in the courtyard of the home after the Christmas story has been read from the Bible. Great emphasis is placed on the manner in which the thorns burn, since this is supposed to foretell the fortune of the house for the coming year. A psalm is sung while the fire is burning, then when the fire is out everybody jumps over the ashes and makes a wish.

And what would Christmas be without music? The custom of having music at Christmas began in the churches hundreds of years ago in the form of litanies. Today every church prepares special Christmas music. Relics of the old-time English waites are the carollers who go about from house to house Christmas Eve or early Christmas morning. If you have ever wakened at dawn on Christmas to hear voices of men and women ringing through the clear cold air in some beautiful old carol such as "Little Town of Bethlehem," or "Silent Night, Holy Night," you will agree that it is a custom well worth keeping. In the Ukraine the major part of Christmas—observed by them on January 7th—is spent in singing carols. Groups of young *kolyakniki* go from house to house singing hymns in praise of the Christ.

In Roumania boys carry bags along with them on their carolling to receive the gifts that are given them. Singers in Poland used to carry a star around with them; sometimes they dressed themselves to represent characters of the Nativity story.

In Spain where the weather is warm on Christmas Day and the whole world seems filled with flowers and music, there is dancing on this Holy Day, for when the Spanish people are happy they dance.

Every nation that celebrates Christmas seems to have some special dish for the Christmas feast. Long ago in Merrie England, boar's head and brawne, peacock and mutton-pies seemed essential to a successful Yule dinner. These mutton-pies were a forerunner of our own mince-meat pies. In Scotland it was the custom for some member of the family to rise before any of the others and prepare breakfast which had to be eaten in bed. Bannocks were

baked for every member of the family; it was believed un
lucky if any of these broke in the oven.

Christmas cakes are popular in every country. The Mora
vians here in America are famous for their thin-as-paper
temptingly delicious Christmas cakes, made in all sizes and
shapes weeks before Christmas. *Pfeffer küchen,* a hard
spice-cake, is popular in Germany. In Denmark the thou
sands of tiny cakes baked for Christmas consumption are
known as pepper nuts. The wafers that the Polish people
make for Christmas, *oplatki,* are stamped with representa
tive religious figures and blessed by the priests. Then they
are given away as gifts and even used as Christmas cards
These wafers also are objects of a ritual performed among
Polish families on Christmas Eve. When the first star
appears in the Christmas sky, each member of the family
breaks the *oplatki* for another, while solemn greetings are
exchanged. *Turté,* a special bread or cake the dough of
which is supposed to represent the swaddling clothes of
the Infant Jesus, are eaten in Roumania, while the Serbian
Christmas cake, called *chestnitsa,* contains a silver coin, and
the one who finds it in his portion is considered fortunate
indeed. Norwegians bake a special rice pudding for the
Yule dinner in which an almond is hidden, and the one
to get the almond will be the first married!

Fish is popular in some of the European countries as a

Christmas dish. In Sweden the biggest and finest fishes of the year are saved for Yule, blessed by the priests and prepared in the special way that only a Swedish housewife knows. At the Christmas feast it is served as *lut-fisk,* the main dish on the table. Other Scandinavian countries also serve fish at their feast, while Italians prefer eels for Christmas, and in Spain sea-bream is eaten by way of a very old custom.

A dish that is served exclusively on Christmas Eve in Mexico has been named for the holy night,—*Ensalada de la Noche Buena.* It is made from a mixture of many fruits and vegetables and garnished with gay-colored candies. The Ukrainian housewife has a big meal to prepare on Christmas Eve, for according to tradition, she must have twelve different kinds of food on the table at the Holy Supper. One of these is the traditional *kutia* partaken of by every member of the family when prayers are said and wishes expressed for the coming year. Then the housewife dashes some of the *kutia* from a spoon into every corner of the house, saying: " May all evil fail to take to our sheep and cattle, as this wheat fails to take to the wall! "

Every good Serb eats roast pig on Christmas Day in honor of *Bozhitch,* an ancient sun god of pagan times who somehow became so closely identified with Christmas traditions that his name in the Serbian language now means Christmas.

In Finland the week before Christmas finds the mother of the house pounding oats for the St. Stephen's Day porridge which all the people eat there on Christmas Day celebrated in that country as the Eve of St. Stephen's.

Christmas dinner for the Shakers, a communitarian sect in the eastern part of the United States, stands out from all other meals of the year, for it is the only time the men and women sit down to a meal together. With the men seated at one side of the long table and the women at the other, the meal is eaten in perfect silence. However, after the Christmas repast, all stand at their places and go through the ceremonious "shaking" dance that has given these people their name. This is probably the most unusual of any Christmas feast in our country.

While speaking of Christmas foods we certainly must not neglect the American roast turkey, the eating of which has become so truly an American custom. Other countries, too, have discovered this delicious fowl introduced to the Pilgrim Fathers three hundred years ago by the Indians. In Mexico it is prepared with *tortillas* and fried peppers. Even in far-off China and Japan the Easterners have adopted turkey as a Christmas dish in those homes where the Yuletide is celebrated.

Yes, Christmas is celebrated in the Orient in many homes and in all of the big cities. Along with Santa Claus whom the Japanese children know as *Hoteiosho*—a god who is always pictured as carrying a pack, and is said to have eyes in the back of his head so he can see the children at all times—and whom the Chinese call *Dun Che Lao Ren*—Christmas Old Man. They even have community trees trimmed with lights and tinsel. In the missionary compounds of India the Christmas tree would certainly surprise American children, for very often it is a banana tree with bananas still growing upon it, and trimmings interlacing the fruit!

The custom of decorating our houses with evergreens at Christmas comes from the Romans. It was considered good luck to exchange branches of green on the Kalends of January; gradually the custom was adopted by those who observed Christmas. With the Druids, those ancient pagans, mistletoe was a token of good luck, possibly because they believed it had great curative powers. Christmas decorations were at first used only in the churches:

> *Holly and Ivy, Box and Bay,*
> *Put in the church on Christmas Day,*

an old rhyme said.

Today the Finnish people " pave the way " for the Christ Child by cutting and piling up great pine boughs, making a huge green carpet from the top of a hill down to the

heart of the village. Then everyone lights "luck chips"—
pinewood tapers that have been buried in the snow for
three days; good luck is supposed to come to those whose
tapers burn well.

The Greek Orthodox Church calls Christmas the Feast
of Lights. As the Light of the World, Christ is represented
in every land by the numerous lights of Christmas: candles,
tapers, lights on the Christmas tree, and stars that are
reminiscent of the Christmas star that shone down on the
shepherds who watched their flocks on that first Holy Night
long ago. In Ireland a tall candle is kept burning in the
window all night to light the Christ Child on His way. A
beautiful custom of the Moravian Church in America is
the traditional candle service held on Christmas Eve
especially for the children. Everyone in the congregation
is given a tiny, lighted beeswax candle in commemoration
of the coming of Christ, the coming of Light into the world.
A child soloist leads the antiphonal musical part of this
impressive service.

In Italy, Spain, Mexico and other countries where the
Yuletide season comes during the warm season, flowers are
used for Christmas decoration instead of evergreens. In
Mexico the *Noche Buena,* a beautiful scarlet plant, is in
full bloom and used profusely for decorating the homes
and churches; while in Australia a red and green Christmas

Bush and the delicate Christmas Bell are in luxuriant growth.

Although we here in America observe only Christmas Eve and Christmas Day, the holiday in many countries lasts much longer. We have seen how the Mexicans observe two full weeks, and the same is true in Spain. In Holland and Belgium St. Nicholas comes December 6th to distribute gifts to the children. Sweden begins to celebrate on December 13th which is St. Lucia's Day, and in Norway the Yule begins on St. Thomas's Day, December 21st and lasts until New Year's. In Ireland, the days from St. Stephen's Eve (December 25th) until Twelfth Night are kept as holidays with little or no work done, while mummers sing their carols to remind people that this is the blessed Christmas time.

Christmas customs in the United States vary according to the sections, depending upon the origin of the people who have settled there. In the valleys of Pennsylvania where the Pennsylvania Dutch have settled there will be found traces of German and Swiss customs. Out in the Middle West, particularly in Minnesota and Wisconsin, the Scandinavians have influenced Christmas observances. But there are some customs that are distinctly American. The Southern States, for example, have a practice of shooting off fireworks on Christmas. Unique, too, is the custom of trimming trees and shrubbery on the lawn with bright electric lights.

Speaking of Santa, our Santa Claus is distinctly an American personality! In other countries he is pictured as a tall dignified saint robed in all the official vestments of a bishop while our patron saint of children is a fat, jolly, countrified looking gentleman defying all the convention of the former Bishop of Myra in his make-up! This purely American type of Santa is due to a great extent to a famous poem written in 1822. Dr. Clement Moore wrote " The Night Before Christmas " for his own children, but when it appeared in print, first in a newspaper and later in a collection of his poetry, it was instantly taken to the hearts of American children everywhere. This jolly St. Nick of reindeer and sleigh and a pack full of toys has brought joy to millions of boys and girls and has been to them for many years the only true Santa Claus. With his description as expressed in the famous poem, we close this story of Christmas.

> *He was dressed all in fur from his head to his foot,*
> *And his clothes were all tarnished with ashes and soot;*
> *A bundle of toys he had flung on his back,*
> *And he looked like a pedlar just opening his pack.*
>
> *His eyes—how they twinkled! his dimples how merry!*
> *His cheeks were like roses, his nose like a cherry!*
> *His droll little mouth was drawn up like a bow,*
> *And the beard of his chin was as white as the snow;*

The stump of a pipe he held tight in his teeth,
And the smoke it encircled his head like a wreath;
He had a broad face and a little round belly,
That shook when he laughed like a bowl full of jelly.

He was chubby and plump, a right jolly old elf,
And I laughed when I saw him, in spite of myself;
A wink of his eye and a twist of his head
Soon gave me to know I had nothing to dread.

He spoke not a word, but went straight to his work,
And filled all the stockings; then turned with a jerk,
And laying his finger aside of his nose,
And giving a nod, up the chimney he rose;

He sprang to his sleigh, to his team gave a whistle,
And away they all flew like the down of a thistle.
But I heard him exclaim, ere he drove out of sight,
HAPPY CHRISTMAS TO ALL AND TO ALL A GOOD
   NIGHT!

OTHER HOLIDAYS

AMERICAN INDIAN DAY
Second Saturday in May

Observed by Arizona, California, Illinois, Minnesota, Montana, New Mexico, New York, South Dakota, Washington and Wisconsin. First celebrated by New York May 13, 1916, it was established for the purpose of recognizing and honoring the American Indian and improving his condition. The President of the American Indian Association, Sherman Coolidge, an Arapahoe Indian, asked that this day be observed " as one set apart as a memorial to the red race of America and to a wise consideration of its future, . . . as a part of the American people." Many changes have taken place in regard to the American Indian as a result of the Indian Reorganization Act of June 18, 1934. In 1936 a secret vote was taken in the tribes in which the Indians were to state whether or not they wished to continue with the tribal form of government. The old law in which Indians were given lands by the Government and then allowed to sell them was abolished. Indian tribal lands may not be sold. There have also been marked improvements in the educational system with an endeavor to give the American Indian vocational training, thereby making him self-supporting.

ARMY DAY
April 6

Named as a holiday by action of the Senate in 1935, though previously observed for many years.

BIRD DAY
Usually second week in April

Often observed with Arbor Day, it was first celebrated in 1894 by the schools of Oil City, Pennsylvania. Started by the National Association of Audubon Societies for the Protection of Wild Birds and Animals, its observance is sponsored by the United States Department of Agriculture.

BOY SCOUT DAY
February 8

This is the anniversary of the founding of the Boy Scouts of America in 1910, and is the first day of Scout

Week, observed by Scouts all over the United States and Possessions.

BRITISH EMPIRE DAY
May 24

This was Queen Victoria's birthday, and though it is distinctly a British holiday, it is observed in the United States by the English population, and universally in Canada where it had its origin.

BUNKER HILL DAY
June 17

Commemorating the Battle of Bunker Hill, at Bunker Hill, Boston, Massachusetts on June 17, 1775. Although this battle was lost to the British it was a " moral victory " giving the colonists confidence, after having seen the British retreat twice. At the site of the battle where Warren was killed stands the Bunker Hill Monument, the cornerstone of which was laid by Lafayette in 1825. It was at this ceremony Daniel Webster made one of the greatest orations of his career. It is a holiday in Boston.

CANDLEMAS
February 2

February 2d is popularly known in America as Ground-Hog Day, but it is also, and more traditionally, Candlemas. The name Candlemas comes from the custom of the blessing of candles by the clergy and their distribution to members of the congregation, one of the most beautiful of all church ceremonies. In the Roman Catholic Church Candlemas is celebrated as the Purification of the Virgin; this festival is also observed in the Greek Catholic Church and the Protestant Episcopal Church. At its beginning, in Jerusalem, the day was known simply as the fortieth day after Epiphany, but in the fourth century the date was changed to February 2d. Beeswax candles are blessed, sprinkled and incensed, then distributed, while the choir sings the antiphon " *Adorna thalamum tuum, Sion,*" the clergy and the laity carry the lighted candles in a solemn march through the church. According to the *Catholic Encyclopedia:* " The solemn procession represents the entry of Christ, who is the Light of the World, into the Temple of Jerusalem."

Candlemas has been for centuries a popular day for weather prognostications, probably originating in the pre-Christian era. An old rhyme said:

If Candlemas day be dry and fair,
The half o' winter's to come and mair;
If Candlemas day be wet and foul,
The half o' winter's gone at Yule.

This was not the only superstition regarding the day. It was considered ill luck to permit the Christmas greens to remain in the house after Candlemas. The snowdrop is known in England as the Candlemas or Purification flower. In Scotland on Candlemas there is a custom of long-standing whereby the children give small gifts of money to their teachers. In Mexico, people think of Candlemas as the time when Christmas celebrations are brought to an end, for Christmas is probably celebrated there more extensively than in any other nation of the world.

Ground-Hog Day originated with the Germans. The idea was brought to America by settlers who held the belief that the badger was a weather prognosticator! In the eastern states where there are no badgers, it is the ground-hog who sees his shadow, or doesn't see it, according to what the weather is on February 2d. If Mr. Ground-Hog finds bright skies when he comes out of his hole and sees his shadow, he withdraws once more to remain for another six weeks, thus retarding spring for that long! On the other hand, if the sky is overcast and the weather is dull throughout the day, Mr. Ground-Hog walks abroad and the sign is portentous! Spring is on its way. In some rural sections this superstition has become so deep-rooted that farmers plan their crops accordingly. In Lancaster County where the Pennsylvania German farmers hold to this belief of their forefathers, there is actually an organization called the Slumbering Groundhog Lodge. A group of farmers from this famous farming center goes through a ritual every year on the second of February to discover what the groundhog does. Depending upon that small animal and his habits, and the sun, they prognosticate the weather of the next six weeks just as their forefathers did many years before them.

CONSTITUTION DAY

September 17

There are three anniversaries of the Constitution of the United States: first, September 17th when it was first adopted by a majority in 1787; second, June 21st when it was established by ratification of the ninth state, New Hampshire, thus making it legal under the terms of the Constitution itself—see Article VII—in 1788; third, March 4, 1789, when it was declared by the Governmental Congress to be in effect.

ELECTION DAY

First Tuesday after the first Monday in November

The time for Election Day was set by an Act of Congress in 1854. It is a legal holiday in all states except Connecticut, Illinois (where it is legal in Chicago), Massachusetts, Mississippi, Ohio and Vermont.

FATHER'S DAY
Third Sunday in June

First celebrated June 19, 1910; originated by Mrs. John Bruce Dodd and sponsored by the Ministerial Association and the Y. M. C. A. of Washington; not so widely observed as Mother's Day.

FIRE PREVENTION DAY
October 9

This date was chosen because the Chicago Fire was on October 8th and 9th in 1871. Since 1911 the first week of October has been observed as Fire Prevention Week.

FOREFATHERS' DAY
December 22

Celebrated by New England Societies everywhere as an anniversary of the landing of the Pilgrims at Plymouth Rock in 1620; observed since 1769.

FRANCES E. WILLARD DAY
Fourth Friday in October

Observed in schools of Tennessee, Kansas and South Dakota.

GROUND-HOG DAY
See Candlemas

JACKSON'S DAY
January 8

Legal in Louisiana. Celebrated by Democrats all over the United States by Jackson Day dinners. The date commemorates Jackson's victory at New Orleans January 8, 1815.

JEFFERSON DAVIS DAY
June 3

Observed by the Southern States. Jefferson Davis, American statesman, was born June 3, 1808; was President of the Confederacy during the Civil War; died 1889.

LABOR DAY
First Monday in September

This is a legal holiday observed to honor Labor. It was inaugurated by the Knights of Labor, an organization founded in Philadelphia in 1869. In 1887 Colorado named May 1st as Labor Day and several other states followed suit, but in 1894 the date was changed permanently to the first Monday in September, and the day became a national holiday. Many countries, however, do observe Labor Day on May 1st, with Labor Union parades and mass meetings. In Australia the day is known as Eight Hour Day, celebrating the shorter working day law. In the United States it is considered as a day of rest and recreation and is generally the end of vacation. Traffic is so heavy over the Labor Day week-end that often there are numerous accidents. Classes in most public schools in the nation begin the following day.

LAFAYETTE DAY

September 6

Celebrated in New York and ten other states; it is also the anniversary of the Battle of the Marne.

LEE'S BIRTHDAY

January 19

Observed by most Southern States. Robert Edward Lee, born January 19, 1807, was a distinguished soldier before the Civil War; asked by Lincoln to take command of the U. S. Army he refused, saying that he could not fight against his mother State of Virginia; took command of the Confederate Army, 1861–65; died 1870. Lee is considered to have been one of the greatest generals the world has ever known.

MARITIME DAY

May 22

This date was chosen in commemoration of the sailing of the *Savannah* from Savannah, Georgia, on May 22, 1819, this being the first successful steam-propelled boat to cross the ocean. The day was named for observance by President Franklin D. Roosevelt when he declared " That May 22d of each year shall hereafter be designated and known as National Maritime Day, and the President is authorized and requested annually to issue a proclamation calling upon the people of the United States to observe such National Maritime Day by displaying the flag at their homes or other suitable places and government officials to display the flag on all government buildings on May 22d of each year."

NAVY DAY

October 27

Observed since 1922, commemorating the birthday of the United States Navy in 1775 when the Congress voted an appropriation of $100,000 to maintain a navy. Also the birthday of Theodore Roosevelt.

PATRIOTS' DAY

April 19

A legal holiday in Massachusetts and Maine, commemorating the Battle of Lexington and Concord on April 19, 1775.

PIONEER DAY
June 15 and June 24

Idaho celebrates this on June 15th as a legal holiday in honor of the first settlement at Franklin, Idaho. It is observed in Wyoming on July 24th with a five-day festival.

SHROVE TUESDAY
Tuesday before Lent

Observed in Alabama, Florida, and Louisiana; as Mardi Gras in New Orleans since 1827; where Germans have settled it is known as *Fastnacht*. Often it is called Pancake Day because of the almost universal custom of eating pancakes on this day.

WHITSUNDAY
Seventh Sunday after Easter

Commemorating the day when the Holy Ghost descended upon the Disciples, this day is observed by all Christian countries of the world. The name comes from the white garb worn by those who are baptized on that day. WHITMONDAY in England is a bank holiday.

DAYS OBSERVED IN ONE STATE ONLY

ARIZONA ADMISSION DAY—*February 14.*

ALASKA DAY—*October 18.*

BATTLE OF BENNINGTON DAY—*August 16* (Vermont).

BATTLE OF NEW ORLEANS DAY—*January 8* (Louisiana).

BATTLE OF SAN JACINTO DAY—*April 21* (Texas).

CALIFORNIA ADMISSION DAY—*September 9.*

COLORADO DAY—*August 1.*

DEFENDERS DAY—*September 12* (Maryland) commemorates Battle of North Point.

DELAWARE DAY—*December 7.* U. S. Constitution ratified, 1787.

EMANCIPATION DAY—*March 22* (Puerto Rico).

FAST DAY—*Last Thursday in April* (New Hampshire).

FORREST'S BIRTHDAY—*July 13* (Tennessee) Birthday of General Bedford Forrest.

FRATERNAL DAY—*October 9* (Alabama).

HALIFAX INDEPENDENCE DAY—*April 12* (North Carolina). Date of passage of Halifax Independence Resolutions.

HOLY THURSDAY—*Thursday before Easter Sunday.* Legal in the Philippines.

MARYLAND DAY—*March 25.*

MECKLENBURG INDEPENDENCE DAY—*May 20* (North

Carolina). Anniversary of the signing of the Declaration of Independence.

MISSOURI DAY—*October 1.*

NEVADA DAY—*October 31.*

PENNSYLVANIA DAY—*March 4.* Anniversary of Penn's Charter, March 4, 1681.

RHODE ISLAND INDEPENDENCE DAY—*May 4.*

SEWARD DAY—*March 30* (Alaska).

TEXAS INDEPENDENCE DAY—*March 2.*

WEST VIRGINIA DAY—*June 20.*

WILSON'S BIRTHDAY—*December 28* (South Carolina). Birthday of Woodrow Wilson.

JEWISH HOLIDAYS AND FAST DAYS

NEW YEAR—*Tishri 1.*

FAST OF GUEDALIAH—*Tishri 3.*

DAY OF ATONEMENT—*Tishri 10.*

TABERNACLES, FIRST DAY—*Tishri 15.*

TABERNACLES, EIGHTH DAY—*Tishri 22.*

REJOICING OF THE LAW—*Tishri 23.*

CHANNUKAH—*Kislev 25.*

FAST OF TEBET—*Tebet 10.*

PURIM—*Adar 14.*

PASSOVER, FIRST DAY—*Nisan 15.*

PASSOVER, SEVENTH DAY—*Nisan 21.*

PASSOVER, LAST DAY—*Nisan 22.*
SHABOUTH, FEAST OF WEEKS—*Sivan 6.*
FAST OF TAMMUZ—*Tammuz 17.*
FAST OF ABH—*Abh 9.*

PRINCIPAL FESTIVALS OF THE ROMAN CATHOLIC CHURCH

CHRISTMAS, EASTER, EPIPHANY, WHITSUNDAY, ASCENSION, CORPUS CHRISTI, THE SACRED HEART, ASSUMPTION, IMMACULATE CONCEPTION, ST. JOHN THE BAPTIST, ST. JOSEPH, SS. PETER and PAUL, ALL SAINTS'.

BIBLIOGRAPHY

Arnadottir, Holmfridur. *When I was a Girl in Iceland.*

Banks, Mrs. M. M. *British Calendar Customs*—Scotland.

Birmingham, G. A., pseud. (Hannay). *Lighter Side of Irish Life.*

Baring-Gould, Rev. S. *Lives of the Saints.*

Beuret, Georgette. *When I was a Girl in France.*

Bianco, Margery Williams. *Paris.*

Brand, John. *Popular Antiquities of Great Britain* (3 volumes).

Brenner, Anita. *Your Mexican Holiday.*

Brewster, H. Pomeroy. *Saints and Festivals of the Christian Church.*

Brockner, Jessie. *Danish Life in Town and Country.*

Butler, Rev. Alban. *Lives of the Saints.*

Carr, Henry. *Old Mother Mexico.*

Catholic Encyclopedia.

Chambers, R., ed. *Book of Days.*

Compton's Pictured Encyclopedia.

Davies, E. C. *A Boy in Serbia.*

Davis, Wm. Stearns. *Life in Elizabethan Days.*

Deems, Edward M., comp. *Holy-Days and Holidays.*

Douglas, George William. *The American Book of Days.*

Dyer, T. F. T. *British Popular Customs.*

Earle, Alice Morse. *Child Life in Colonial Days.*

Eddy, Floyd Champlin. *Holidays.*

Eichler, Lillian. *Customs of Mankind.*

Encyclopedia Americana.

Encyclopedia Britannica.

Federal Writers' Project on W. P. A. *A South Dakota Guide.*

Fowler, W. Warde. *Roman Festivals.*

Franciscan Almanac.

Guaranty Trust Company. *Bank and Public Holidays Throughout the World.*

Gunsaulus, Helen C. *Japanese New Year's Festival, Games and Pastimes.*

Haldane, Elizabeth S. *The Scotland of our Fathers.*

Hall, Dr. J. O. *When I was a Boy in Norway.*

Hamilton, Schuyler. *History of the National Flag of the U. S. of A.*

Harrison, Peleg. *Stars and Stripes.*

Hogg, Philip, comp. *A Calendar of Old English Customs Still in Being*, 1936.

Hone, Wm. *Every-day Book.*

Howitt, Wm. *Rural Life in England.*

Humphrey, Grace. *Stories of the World's Holidays.*

Iwadō, Tamotsu. *Children's Days in Japan.*

Kane, Joseph Nathan. *Famous First Facts.*

Kelley, Ruth Edna. *Book of Hallowe'en.*

Knowlson, T. Sharper. *Origins of Popular Superstitions and Customs.*

Library of War Literature. *A Declaration of Interdependence.*

Lincoln Library of Essential Information.

Long, George. *Folklore Calendar.*

Love, W. DeLoss. *The Fast and Thanksgiving Days of New England.*

McDonald, Etta B. & Dalrymple, Julia. *Boris in Russia.*

McDonald, Etta Blaisdell. *Colette in France.*

McDonald, Etta B. & Dalrymple, Julia. *Gerda in Sweden.*

McSpadden, J. Walker. *The Book of Holidays.*

Miles, Clement A. *Christmas.*

Mooney, James. *Holiday Customs in Ireland.*

Moss, James A. *Flag of the United States, its History and Symbolism.*

Orne, Martha Russell. *Hallowe'en.*

Our Holidays; retold from *St. Nicholas.*

Patten, Helen Plubrook. *Year's Festivals.*

Pattison, S. Louise. *When I was a Girl in Switzerland.*

Popular Italian Costumes, Music, Dances and Festivals.

Pringle, M. P. & Urann, C. A. *Yuletide in Many Lands.*

Purnell, Idella. *Little Yusuf.*

Robson, E. J. *A Guide to French Fêtes.*

Schauffler, Robert H., ed. *Our American Holidays—Series.*

Sechrist, Elizabeth Hough. *Christmas Everywhere.*

Sechrist, Elizabeth Hough. *Little Book of Hallowe'en.*

Sidgwick, Mrs. Alfred. *Germany.*

Spicer, Dorothy Gladys. *Book of Festivals.*

Tillie, Alexander. *Yule and Christmas: Their Place in the Germanic Year.*

Treble, H. A. & King, K. M. *Every Day Life in Rome.*

Trevelyan, Marie. *Glimpses of Welsh Life and Character.*

U. S. Department of Agriculture. *Arbor Day, its Purpose and Observance.*

U. S. Department of Agriculture. *Famous Trees.*

U. S. George Washington Bi-Centennial Commission. *History of the U. S. George Washington Bi-Centennial Commission.*

Van Teslaar, James S. *When I was a Boy in Roumania.*

Viski, Karoli. *Hungarian Peasant Customs.*

Walsh, William Shepard. *Curiosities of Popular Customs.*

Warren, Nathan B. *The Holidays: Christmas, Easter, and Whitsuntide.*

Wilstack, Paul. *An Italian Holiday.*

Winlow, Clara V. *Our Little Servian Cousin.*

World Almanac.

World Book Encyclopedia.

Wright, A. R. *British Calendar Customs 1938.*

INDEX

(*See pages 237, 238 for holidays observed in one State only.*)

A

All Saints' Day, 183–187
  in Wales, 184

All Souls' Day, 183–187
  in England, 184, 185
  " France, 185
  " Lithuania, 185
  " Mexico, 186
  " Poland, 186
  " Portugal, 185
  " Wales, 184

American Indian Day, 226

April Fools' Day, 89–95
  in England, 90, 92, 94
  " France, 91–93
  " India, 93
  " Portugal, 93
  " Scotland, 92

Arbor Day, 96–106
  in England, 98
  " Germany, 98
  " Hawaii, 98
  " Japan, 98
  " Palestine, 98
  " Spain, 98

Army Day, 227

Armistice Day, 188–195
  "Great Silence" of, 194
  in churches, 193
  made legal, 193
  signed, 188

Ascension Day, 85

Ash Wednesday, 81

B

Bastile Day, 164

Befana, La, 213

Bird Day, 96, 227

Boy Scout Day, 227

British Empire Day, 228

Bunker Hill Day, 228

Burbank, Luther, birthday, 96

C

Calendar, ancient Egyptian, 15, 28
  ancient German, 16
  Gregorian, 21, 22, 28, 90
  Hebrew, 22, 23